OUR BIRD BOOK

OUR
BIRD BOOK

Sydney Rogerson
and
Charles Tunnicliffe

COLLINS
14 ST. JAMES'S PLACE LONDON

TEXT PRINTED BY THE PUBLISHERS
AT CATHEDRAL STREET, GLASGOW
COLOUR PLATES PRINTED BY
BEMROSE AND SONS LTD. DERBY
1947

Contents

A STOAT

6

Illustrations in Colour

Illustrations in black and white

Dedication

TO JANE

Often when we have had our talks about birds you have asked me to get you a book which would tell you things about them—the difference between a song-thrush and a mistle-thrush, perhaps, or why the tawny owl hooted round the house at night, or how the martins set about building their mud homes above your bedroom window. I hunted around, but I could not find the sort of book which I thought you would like, and which would give you real pictures of our bird friends and acquaintances. Then I talked to Uncle Charles, and he said if I would write a book he would do the pictures. So together we have made this book for you, for your friends, and for all who already love birds, or who would soon grow to love them if they knew what interesting, delightful and beautiful people they are.

SYDNEY ROGERSON

Barningham,
Suffolk.

11

MISTLE THRUSH
SONG THRUSH

Chapter I

BIRDS IN GENERAL

WHEREVER you live—in a town, in the country, or at the seaside—you will see birds. You will see them every day, and hear them singing or chirping or calling to one another on most days. You see them and you hear them, but do you notice them? Do you know them? Can you tell one bird from another? I wonder. Birds are most lovely creatures. Of course, there are birds which are ugly, like the vulture, with his bald head and scraggy neck. But there are no vultures in Great Britain, so you need not bother about them. Nearly all the birds in our country are lovely in their shape or in the colour of their feathers. One or two are comical. I think the funniest is the puffin. Here he is, for all the world like a fat little old man with a swollen nose! You will not see puffins unless you live at the seaside, and then only in certain parts of the British Isles. In this book I am not going to bother you with rare or out-of-the-way birds. I want you to get to know those you may hope to see almost any day. Of course, birds which are quite common where you are living may be uncommon where I live. When I was a boy my home was in a corner of the Yorkshire dales, where almost any day I could see or hear grouse or curlew or ring-ouzels, which I never saw at all when I grew up and went to live in Huntingdonshire and Suffolk. But there I found birds which I had never seen before. Blackcaps and goldfinches made their nests in the garden, and we could watch yellow-eyed stone-curlews running about in the heather. And if we went only a short distance away we might, if we were lucky, catch a glimpse of a funny whiskery little bird called a bearded tit-mouse, swaying about in the tall reeds at the edge of river or lake. So some of the birds which are regular friends to you may be exciting strangers to lots of other people. But, wherever we live, there will be birds which we shall be able to watch every day—sparrows, robins, blackbirds and thrushes, chaffinches and rooks.

Let's begin by taking a look at one or two of them. A robin, for example.

You must know him, and what a fit, perky small person he is, with his fat, red tummy, and shining black eyes. He looks the picture of health and happiness as he cocks his head first to one side and then the other. Or that sparrow. Watch him as he fairly bounces along wall or pavement looking for something to eat. If you look closely you will see that he jumps off the ground with both feet at once, so that he moves forward in what, for a small thing like him, are big leaps. You try and do it, and see how difficult and tiring it is! Seeing them, you will think what fit and happy people birds are, and you will be right. When they are well, when they have had enough food and sleep, they show how they enjoy life by singing and flying and hopping briskly about. But what I want you to realise is that though they are so happy and carefree, they are weak things for whom life can be very hard. They have many enemies, and only one real friend—and that is you.

Every minute of their lives the smaller birds must be on the watch for the animals and other and bigger birds which are trying to kill them to eat. They can trust no one. First, there is your cat, which will stalk them and pounce upon them just as fiercely as she will upon a mouse. She will even climb the trees to steal on them as they sit asleep, with their heads tucked under one wing. Cruel brutes like stoats and weasels are after them day and night, and squirrels, especially the grey ones, rats, and even mice, will rob their nests to eat their eggs and their babies. They have enemies even among other birds. In the daytime, crows and hawks may hunt them and their families; and at night, hungry owls fly about looking for a supper of little birds. And, of course, there are thoughtless boys and girls, and even grown-ups, who steal their eggs and break up the lovely nests which have been built with so much labour and skill and care.

Yet birds know, I think, that most boys and girls are their friends. How else can we explain why it is that so many of our ordinary small birds choose to build their nests in our gardens? They do. They seem to feel that the closer they come to you and me the safer they will be from their other enemies, who are our enemies too. That is why those of us who have gardens should make them as safe as we can for birds, and even help the birds by making boxes for them to build their nests in. The birds will soon know, and you will be surprised to find how pleased they will be. They will show their gratitude by coming more and more to build their homes close to yours. My garden is full of nests, and I try and look after them. Yet how few birds bring up their families. I find one nest after another, watch it till it has one egg, two, three, or four. Then I come back in a day or two, and find either the eggs gone or sometimes the whole nest smashed up. Or I may watch till the mother-bird has hatched out her babies, and then find that some cat, or rat, or robber bird, has taken them all. This makes me angry, and I am glad when I know that a whole brood has safely grown up and flown away.

But what, you will ask, about the bigger and fiercer birds which kill and

CHAFFINCH

GREENFINCH

VULTURE

PUFFIN

ROBIN

eat the smaller ones? They also are lovely, but in a different way. They have a wild beauty, such as you will find in a lion or a tiger or leopard at the Zoo, or even in your own cat. You may not like it as much, but if you are lucky enough to get a close view of a hawk or an owl or a jay you will see what I mean. Look at the graceful wings and head of a hawk, the wise furriness of an old owl, or the cheeky crest and bright colours of the jay. It is not their wish to be cruel. Nature made them eat other birds or their eggs. Because of this, their chief enemy is you and me. These killer and robber birds are killed by us to keep them from becoming so common that they do too much damage, and men with guns or traps are even worse enemies than the animal enemies of the small birds. Which is why the bigger birds usually go as far as they can from our houses and make their nests in wild places. The biggest and fiercest and handsomest of all, the great golden eagle, may now only be found in the loneliest mountains of Scotland. He has been driven there by men.

TAWNY-OWL

The weather is another hard enemy. When winter sets in with its snow and storms and ice you and I put on our woollies and feel fine. In the hot days of summer we change into thin clothes, and on very hot days probably find some lake or the sea to paddle and bathe in. In winter we have fires in our houses and warming food, and in summer we take cool drinks and pull down blinds to keep out the sun. Birds can do none of these things. They have just the same feathers winter and summer, and they feel the cold dreadfully. Watch them as they sit sadly in snow-time with their feathers all fluffed up, as if to pretend to themselves that they have put on more clothes. I should perhaps explain that, besides being so active and full of energy, birds have higher temperatures than we have, and so must be constantly eating something if they are to keep "on the go." Birds like the chaffinch and sparrow live on seeds and such-like things, the blackbird and thrush eat fruit and worms and snails. In winter, when snow covers the ground or frost hardens it, they can neither find seeds nor pull worms out of the earth. At such times you can do a lot to help them. In winter you can throw out some

food every day, the crumbs off the breakfast-table, or some odd pieces of cheese rind. If the snow is on the ground, you must be careful to sweep a place clear, so that the scraps don't fall into the snow where the birds cannot reach them. If you wish to add to your own enjoyment and knowledge of birds, the best plan is to make, or get someone to make for you what is called a bird-table. This need be no more than a flat piece of wood on a post, but it should be put somewhere where you can see it conveniently from a window, so that you can watch without moving about too much, and so frightening the birds from it. Also you should make it so that you can hang pieces of bacon fat or cheese rind down towards it from a string. This is to attract the tits, who seem to prefer to eat standing on their heads. They will alight on the piece of bacon or cheese, swaying at the end of the string, and then proceed to peck at it from the bottom with their tails in the air! If you have a bird-table you will soon see the natures of the different birds. Almost as soon as you have put food on it the bold birds—like sparrows, robins, tits, and chaffinches—will come to eat, but the shyer birds will take a long time to get used to it, and only approach very gradually, looking about them most suspiciously as they do so. In summer you will help by putting out a dish or pan of water, for when the weather is really dry, birds find it hard to get enough to drink or to bath in and sometimes have to make very long journeys in search of water.

Although birds are affected by very hot dry weather, they all love the sun. Their whole lives depend on it, and on the light and warmth it gives. Long before you and I are awake, even before the first pale gleam of dawn pierces the darkness of night, birds climb into the sky to be ready to greet the sun. And just before it begins to light the earth they salute it with the dawn chorus. Some summer morning, every one of you must manage just once to wake early before it is light and wait to hear that wonderful burst of bird-song. I shall never forget the first time I heard it. I was on board a little sailing yacht moored in the Beaulieu river in Hampshire. Something had wakened me and I got up and went on deck. It was dark and very still. The cool breeze ruffled my hair and the tide lapped and gurgled round the boat. All at once a bird began to sing far away. One or two more joined in, until, suddenly, with a crash, every bird within miles burst into song. The sky rang with music from thousands of throats. For perhaps twenty minutes the chorus lasted, then, as the day broke, died swiftly away. I thought, somehow, of hundreds of school choir-boys finishing an anthem, and immediately rushing to take off their surplices to start the day's work. That, I knew, was what the birds were doing. They had saluted the returning sun. Now they had to set about the day's hard tasks of nest-building and of finding enough food for themselves and their babies. Still, much as birds love the sun, young birds cannot stand much hot sunshine, especially before they get their feathers. When baby birds hatch out of the egg most of them are quite naked and rather hideous, and it is

O.B.B.   c

GREAT TIT
BLUE TIT
COAL TIT
LONG-TAILED TIT

some days before they begin to grow feathers. I know a fly-catcher, a little grey bird, which makes her nest in dead ivy on a wall. She is not afraid to sit there and watch me as I work nearby. When the sun is very hot she covers her four babies, stretching out her wings like a parasol. But she is so hot herself, poor dear, that she sits panting with her beak wide open and her heart beating fast. Birds love a cool bath on a hot day. One clever bird-watcher tells how she once watched a chiff-chaff—which is one of our smaller summer visitors—having a shower-bath. There had been a heavy dew in the night, and a clump of tall flowers was drenched with water. The chiff-chaff flew down from a tall tree and landed plonk on the flowers, which, of course, covered him with a shower of spray each time he did it! You may not have the luck to see anything like that, but if you know some small pond or pool, and have the patience to sit down and keep quite still, you can have great fun watching how the different birds come to drink and wash themselves. Some will behave in a decent, orderly manner, and patiently wait their turn to drink or bath. Others will push and elbow their way in and cause all sorts of fights.

The smaller birds are apt to wilt and die rather easily. The bigger birds, of course, are stronger and better able to take care of themselves, but hunger or thirst will drive them to come too close to farms and villages, so that they are more easily trapped and shot.

To understand how birds feel cold and heat, you should know that more than half our birds do not stay with us all the year round, but are visitors. Some come in winter. They fly down from the cold frozen countries of the North —like Norway, Sweden, or Russia—to spend the winter with us where it is not so cold and they can find food in the fields on most days. As soon as the spring

JAY

SPARROW-HAWK

GOLDEN EAGLE

comes and warmth begins to return, off they go North again to build their nests, lay their eggs, and bring up their families. As they leave us, other birds begin to arrive. These are birds from the South, from Africa, and they travel to escape from the terrific heat of the African summer, which burns up everything. They come to build their homes in this green and pleasant land of ours, where it is not too hot for young birds and where there is usually plenty for them to find to eat. My fly-catcher is one of the many birds which travel from Africa each spring, but the one you probably know best is the

THRUSH IN THE SNOW

cuckoo—by his cry if not by sight. He is only with us for about five months at the most. You know the rhyme:

> In April come he will,
> In May he sing all day,
> In June he change his tune,
> In July away he fly,
> In August go he must.

His is a very short stay, just about the shortest of all our visitors, and I like to think of Mr. and Mrs. Cuckoo as a fussy old couple, who take great care of their health and are anxious to be away to the Sunny South before the faintest nip of autumn is in the air! But just think of the long journey, over sea and land, that these birds make each year. If we want to go to Norway we go on board a comfortable ship at Newcastle or Hull. The journey takes thirty-six hours, so we have our meals and go to bed and sleep just as we do at home. If we wish to go to Africa by the same route as the birds we have to cross the English Channel in one steamer, then a whole day's railway journey across France; and lastly, another long sea voyage of at least twelve hours. Imagine the thousands of tiny birds which set out to make these journeys with only their wings to bear them over the waste of waters and to beat a way for them against wind and storm. The golden-crested wren—the smallest of all our birds—actually has the pluck and the strength to fly to us across the North Sea, and the gentle chiff-chaff and willow-wren manage somehow to struggle year by year from Africa. Do you wonder that countless numbers find their strength fails them, and fall into the angry waves, or wearily into

STARLING BATHING

the traps set for them by horrid people in Europe; or that others somehow reach the shores of England, only to fall on our beaches to die of exhaustion or to be eaten by sea-birds or animals. It is wonderful that any should manage to arrive at all; but every year a high proportion do get through, to gladden our eyes and ears with their beauty and songs during the months of spring and summer.

Birds are very brave. Only the hawks and owls and big birds like the raven or crow have got beaks and claws which are fit for use as weapons. The smaller birds have nothing with which to fight. Yet many will show great pluck, especially in trying to protect their eggs or young ones. They will not move from their nest sometimes until you touch them, and when they at last fly off they will stay fluttering anxiously about close-by till you have gone away. A minute thing like a blue-tit will peck savagely at your hand if you try and interfere with her nest while she is in it. A mother duck, whose beak is not even as sharp as a hens, will rush at a dog or a cat which goes too near her ducklings, and I have seen many a dog run away from such an angry mother.

Some birds have beautiful feathers, which we call their plumage, and others have beautiful songs. The odd thing is that the birds with bright

AN UNFLEDGED SPARROW

LAPWING SWOOPING

plumage can scarcely ever sing. The most brilliant of all British birds is the kingfisher. If you are lucky you may see him flashing like a pink and blue jewel over the water of pond, lake, or river. He doesn't sing at all. The best he can do is a thin whistle. Compare him with the nightingale, such a dull, plain, greyey-brown bird, who is so shy that you will seldom see him, and if you did see him you would not bother about him unless you knew a lot about birds. Yet he has one of the loveliest songs of all our birds. He sings at night as well as by day. Perhaps when you are in bed one summer evening you may hear the most thrilling, gurgly sort of song coming out of the darkness, and you will know it is the nightingale sitting in a patch of brambles singing to his wife as she sits on her eggs in her nest.

There are all sorts of things to learn about even the commonest bird. One thing you must know is that they belong to different families. Ducks, for instance. There are all sorts of ducks. First, the tame ducks you see in the farmyard. These ordinary white ones, big fat chaps, are called Aylesburys, after a town in Buckinghamshire where they were first bred. The commonest kind of wild duck is known as the mallard. You can tell these because the drake is a handsome bird, with his shiny, black-green head, and the purple patch on his wings, and the duck is a dull person, with only the same purple patches on her wings to let you know which she is. There are many other kinds of British wild ducks. Some are just ducks like the Aylesbury or the mallard, which paddle about on land and swim on the water, where they up-end themselves till you can only see their tails, while their beaks are under water trying to gobble up water-snails and other odd things which they like to eat. Others are diving-ducks, which seldom come out on land, because their legs are so short that they are not good walkers. But they are wizards in the water. One moment you see them floating about. Then, presto, they are gone!

TUFTED DRAKE

You will watch for them to bob up where they went down, but you will be wrong. They will suddenly appear yards away. They can swim under water far better than they can walk on land. But all ducks, no matter how different their shape, colour, and habits, all belong to the duck family.

Now, why have I told you this? Because, when you see a lot of black birds in a field, you probably say, "Oh, look at those blackbirds!" There are many different birds with feathers which look black, but only one is known as a blackbird, and he belongs to the thrush family. And even then only the cock blackbird is black, with a fine orange beak. His wife is a lady in sober brown. His first cousin is the thrush, the brown speckled-breasted bird which you cannot help seeing somewhere almost every day. The other black-looking birds will probably be rooks, and they belong to the family or tribe of crows. The crows are quite different people from the thrushes—as different as a rabbit is from a rat. The rabbit belongs to the same family as the rat, but the rabbit

DUCK AND DRAKE MALLARD

is a vegetable-eater, and though he may eat your cabbages and lettuces if he gets into your garden, he does no harm to any other animal. His cousin, the rat, is a horrid brute, and will eat bird's eggs, young birds, or anything that comes his way or that he can steal. The blackbird, like his cousins the thrushes, is a decent sort of fellow. He eats worms and snails and things, and if he sometimes likes a meal of fruit—he is as fond of raspberries and currants as the rabbit is of cabbages and lettuces—he does no harm to other birds. And you can forgive the thrushes a lot because they sing so beautifully. Not so the crows. Like the rats, the crows are nasty creatures. They are quite happy to squawk and croak and they eat all sorts of things. The commonest bird of the crow family is the rook. You cannot miss him. For one thing he has a bald face. For another, he always goes about in crowds. The truth is that he cannot bear to be alone. When spring comes, and birds start making their nests, most of them like to get away and build their homes privately. The bald-faced rooks delight to make their nests as close together as possible, which is why you will see a clump of trees full of big, clumsy nests; and what a cawing and a shouting there is as the rooks build them! Those of you who live near a rookery, as it is called, will know the din that goes on. You would not think that there were any rules of behaviour among them, but there are. If one rook—all the crow family are robbers by nature—is lazy and thinks that he will "pinch" for its own nest the sticks and twigs collected by another rook, the others set about the thief and drive it away to live by itself. Which is why you may often see a pair of rooks making a nest on their own, far from a rookery. This is not because they wish to do so, but because they are bad rooks who have been driven out by their friends and relations.

Most of our birds which belong to the crow family are black—that is to say, they look black at a distance, for the surprising thing is that no bird's feathers are really black. You have only to hold what you think is a black feather up to the sun to see the way it shines with all sorts of purple, blue, or green lights. The rook and the jackdaw both look black, though the jackdaw, which is smaller than the rook, has a greyish head. The carrion crow—a very nasty customer—also looks black, but you will seldom see him. He lives in wild, far-away places. But some crows are quite highly-coloured. The magpie, most cunning of all thieves among our birds, is a handsome creature, with his black and white plumage and long tail. The jay, just as nasty a robber, but far shyer than our other crows, is pinky-brown, with a crest on his head and a brilliant little patch of blue and black feathers on his wings. These feathers are often used as ornaments in men's and women's hats.

Another large family of birds are the finches. Most of our finches are handsome. You are sure to know the perky chaffinch. He is easy to recognise with his gay plumage and his sharp cry.

Other large families of every-day birds are the tits, the warblers, the buntings, the game-birds, the waders, the hawks, to name but a few. A few

BULLFINCHES

GOLDFINCHES

birds have no relations in the British Isles. The kingfisher is the only member of his family among our birds, so is the cuckoo, and so, curiously enough, is the common old Cockney sparrow.

PART OF A ROOKERY

Chapter II

FAMILIAR FRIENDS

NOW let us take a close-up look at the birds we can all call everyday-
friends, those we may see round the house or in the garden or the park.
Because he is an oddity, and because he is just as much at home in big
city or little hamlet, let's begin with the sparrow. Everyone knows the sparrow.
You cannot get away from him. You can see him hopping about calmly amid
the roaring traffic of London streets, dodging buses or taxis without seeming
to hurry himself. You can see him bouncing about the grass of cricket ground
or town park, hoping to find a crumb or two left in the paper bags in which
someone brought buns or sandwiches. You can see him taking a dust-bath
in a country lane or sitting cheeping on the thatched roof of a farmhouse. He
is so common that we take him for granted as a cheeky little nuisance,
but if you look at him carefully you will see he is really rather a
handsome fellow. A nuisance he certainly can be and often is. He is mis-
chievous by nature, and because there are so many sparrows they can be most
destructive. Also he often prefers to build his nest in the chimney
or gutter of your house instead of in a tree or wall—and a great big clumsy
bag of a nest it is which blocks up chimney or gutter, causing fires to
smoke and rain-water to overflow. It looks far too big for so small a bird,
but that is because it is just a loosely packed mixture of long straws and grass
lined with lots of soft feathers.

The sparrow used to be included in the finch family, but now his nearest
relatives are thought to be the weaver-birds, which live in India and Africa.
Funnily enough, these birds make their nests neatly out of big leaves, sewing
them by using grasses as thread and their beaks as needles. Mrs. Sparrow sometimes decides it is too much trouble to make her own nest, and then she behaves
very badly. She just sits up in the gutter above the eaves where a pair of
house-martins are building their cosy little round home, about which I will
tell you later. As soon as she sees they have finished it she calls Mr. Sparrow,

26

and together they drive away the poor house-martins and take the nest for themselves! Sparrows lay from four to six eggs, and may lay two or three times each year. The eggs are a shiny greyish-white, with grey, greyey-brown, or nearly black spots.

Everyone of you must know the familiar robin, which we have already mentioned. What you may not know is that he is a distant relation of the blackbird, being a small member of the large family of thrushes. He has lots of close relations scattered about the world, some of which come to us as summer visitors, and which we shall come to later on. In Europe the robin is a shy bird, haunting the wild woods and forests, but here he is friendly to the point of boldness. In fact he is altogether rather a pushing person, determined to miss nothing. Like the sparrow, he likes to live near our homes, so that he can note everything we do. Almost as soon as you open the door to go out he will appear as if from nowhere and sit watching, hoping you will throw him some crumbs, or perhaps go and dig in the garden, and so give him a chance to find a few fat grubs or worms in the freshly turned earth. For all his nice looks he is a bad-tempered little fellow, and will fight fiercely with other robins to win and keep his wife. There are two rather nice things about the robin. First, he is the most all-the-year-round singer of our birds. He has only a small, thin song, but, like the noise made by the cricket on Uncle Arly's nose, it is a " cheerious measure," and he utters it sometime in practically every month of the year. Secondly, robins have a pleasant habit of choosing queer places in which to nest. Perhaps this is because they are so bad tempered that they cannot live close to other birds. They may make their nests in a hole in a wall or in ivy, but they are just as likely to put it in an old boot, or a thrown-away pot or pan or bucket. It's always worth while in springtime—the robin nests early, in March or April—to look into all the broken crocks which lie in the bushes or beds of nettles. You may well be rewarded by finding the neat nest made of mosses lined with hair, and with four or five pretty whitish eggs with reddy-brown spots. Another thing about the robin is that where he was born there he stays, unless or until another robin drives him away. I have one which makes its nest almost underneath a table on which I put food for the birds. He is never late for a meal! If you are patient, you have a better chance of making friends with a robin than most other birds.

Nearly every garden or public park has its blackbirds and thrushes. To give them their proper names, they are the blackbird, the song-thrush and the mistle-thrush. We have already seen that the first two are gentle birds which sing charmingly. I think the blackbird has the richer song of the two, and likes to pour it out towards the close of a spring or summer day, but the thrush has more notes. Indeed, he has possibly more tricks and variations of song than any of our birds. Compared with these two the mistle-thrush is a poor performer as a songster, but he has one thing in his favour—the wilder and more blustery the weather the more he will sing, and for that reason is often known

BEARDED TITS

as the "stormcock." Before a storm or at the height of a gale you may see him perched high in the swaying branches of a tall tree, singing with all his might and main. It is not a very long or lovely song, but it is loud and gay. The mistle-thrush is slightly bigger than the song-thrush, and the spots on his tummy are bigger and fewer. He looks more truculent, and so he is, with none of the gentleness of his songster cousin. Perhaps it will best help you to recognise one from the other if I call him a greyey bird and the song-thrush a browny one. One interesting thing about thrushes is the neat way they have of eating snails. The bird will hunt up a snail and carry it off in its beak to a big stone or a brick, against which it will whack the shell until it is smashed up so that the snail can be picked out and eaten. If you watch, you will probably find that each thrush has a special stone it uses for this purpose, and

HOUSE SPARROWS

around which will be lots of broken snail shells. The thrush family are treasures for anyone who is just beginning to watch birds, because their nests are so easy to find. They nest early, as early as March, and sometimes before the trees are properly covered with leaves, and often choose evergreen bushes like holly or yew or laurel. But they don't seriously worry about hiding their nests, which are biggish, ugly affairs, and would, anyway, be difficult to conceal. But if they are ugly they are very strong. They are well built, with a mortar made of mud or dung mixed in with the grass and straw to make a really hard shell. The song-thrush goes one better, and even finishes its nest off with a smooth lining of dung. The trouble about that, of course, is that the nest is like a cocoanut-shell cup. It holds water, so that if there is a heavy shower while Mrs. Song-Thrush is away, she may come back to find her nursery has become a bath!

Many of you will already know the egg of the song-thrush—a lovely blue one with small black spots. It was the first egg I knew when I was a small boy, and each year I get the same joy when I find my first thrush's nest. It is a sign that spring has come to drive away the gloom and cold of winter. The blackbird's egg is also pretty but not so clean looking. It is more greeney-blue and more thickly covered with sandy-brown spots. The mistle-thrush, whose nest is usually difficult to reach because it is built high up in a tree, has a queer-coloured egg—a sort of grey-blue, with varied spots of purple and blue-black.

Now let's talk about two other birds we should be able to see every day—the starling and the wren. At a distance you'd probably say the starling was another of the blackbirds. He isn't. He may sometimes look black, but get close to him and you will see his plumage shines with bright lights, reds and blues and greens, as the sun strikes it. His is a coat of many colours flecked

BLACKBIRD

with points of white, and a truly handsome fellow he is. The pity is that he is not quite as nice in his habits as in his looks. He is an impudent customer. Although in winter-time you may see single starlings pushing round your bird-table or driving smaller birds away from the food you have thrown out, and although he makes his nest on his own, in holes in trees or in old buildings, he likes to move about in huge crowds, especially in the autumn. Starlings choose special clumps of trees or small copses where they go to sleep at night, and if you happen to live near one of these, on a November afternoon, just as the sun begins to wane, you may see hundreds upon hundreds of starlings flying back to roost. The air is black with them, so that it looks as if someone had upset a pailful of tea-leaves in the sky, and as the birds come in they shout and chatter. Some of them settle at once; others settle and then begin flying round again, and all the time there are bursts of noisy, excited talk. Then as the sun sinks the noise grows less, till as the sky begins to dim it dies away, the hundreds of voices become quieter until all are silent. In olden days these flocks of starlings were called "murmurations," and those of you who have heard the sound they make will know what a good description that is. But starlings are dirty things, and the droppings from a large congregation of them may sooner or later kill the trees in which they roost. Also the starling is one of the few birds which not even a hungry cat will eat. The egg is a lovely pale blue, very pale, with no spots at all.

> "Of all the birds that rove and sing near dwellings made by men,
> None is so nimble, feat and trim as Jenny Wren."

And so say I! The wren is one of my special favourites. I love him. He is such a small compact person, his head and body looking as if they were all of a piece and his tail cocked absurdly over his back. He is a busy little chap, always going and coming, fussing about, taking not the least notice of you and me, but never seeming bold or familiar like a robin or sparrow. This is because the wren is an insect-eater and is everlastingly on the hunt for grubs, and flies and things for himself and for his large family. Tiny bird though it is, the wren lays a big egg for its size—a whitish one, with a few small brown spots—and lays a lot of them too, from five to eight or more. It lays two lots a year. Now there are not so many wrens about, which goes to show you how few birds grow up from all the eggs that are laid. The cock-wren has also got a large-sized voice for so small a person, and has quite a pleasant song. But your joy in watching the busy antics of the wren and learning its song will be still greater when you find its nest. You can look for it almost anywhere low down—stuck against the trunk of a tree, towards the bottom of a hedge, in a hole in the wall, in the ivy or a haystack, even in the brussel sprouts or broccoli—but it is usually so cleverly hidden and camouflaged that you will find it difficult to see even when your nose is close to it. For one thing, it is, a domed nest—that is, it is made like a ball with a neat hole in the side, the cosiest of homes, with even a sort of porch over the hole so that rain cannot drive in. It is beautifully made of leaves or mosses or bracken chosen to match the surroundings in which it is placed. If you find one in April or May you should always be careful how you feel inside it. You will need long fingers to reach down and see if there are any eggs, and you may easily make the hole bigger. The mother bird will know at once, and may quite likely say to herself: "This house has been found by some stranger who may steal my babies. I'd better leave it for their sakes and try somewhere else." The surprising thing is how quickly she is able to find and collect the hundreds of leaves, pieces of moss and feathers, and work them into so cunning a nest. One year a tree in my garden blew down. That was on a Wednesday, but on the Sunday, lo and behold, a wren had built a nest in the roots! A curious thing is that you are likely to find two or three empty nests for each one that has eggs in it. Why this should be is a bit of a mystery. Some people say it is

LAPWING AND CHICKS

STARLING SINGING

PART OF A STARLING ROOST

because the cock wren wants to show what a good husband he is and so makes a nest to show his wife. She may not approve his efforts, so he goes off and makes another. Still she may not like it, and then decides to do the job herself. But I think the reason is that the wren likes comfort—he looks as if he did—and does not see at all why he should not have his own home to go to in the rain and snow of winter when other birds have to sit huddled up and drenched and cold in branches or under eaves. They make these extra nests for their shelter. I think this must be right, because I have accidentally turned wrens out of all sorts of comfy hide-outs. The funniest was one summer evening when a thunderstorm was brewing. I had several bunches of onions hanging to dry on an outhouse wall. I dashed out to put them indoors before they got wet, and as I took down each bunch out flew a young wren! The best way to tell whether the nest you have found is meant for a nursery or a hotel is by the lining. Only those which will have eggs will be softly lined with feathers; the others will just be lined with dried leaves. One thing about the wren that I only learnt the other day made me love him more than ever. As you might imagine, he has lots of pluck and is quite ready to fight. The lovely thing is that as he fights he sings loudly at his enemy! There's a complete little happy warrior for you. "A tiny, inch-long, eager, ardent, feathered mouse!" A great English poet wrote: "He who shall hurt the little wren shall never be beloved by Man."

WRENS.

Another small familiar friend is the hedge-sparrow. It's a poor name, because he is not related to the sparrow at all, and why he should be so called I have never understood. He doesn't look in the least like a sparrow, and he certainly does not behave like one. He is most modest and retiring, so that though he is one of the commonest of our garden dwellers, preferring to live close to our houses, you will scarcely notice him until your eyes become trained. He never comes much into the open if he can help it, but shuffles about in the hedges, in the shrubbery, under the gooseberry bushes, or leaves of the cabbage patch. This is not so much because he wishes to remain out of sight, but because in these places he can best find the grubs and insects he feeds on, and, like all birds, he is a hungry being, having always to be on the hunt for food. But though you may not see much of him you will hear him, for he has a sweet little song, into which he will burst at any time of the day, or even at night, if some noise or light wakes him up. Because he is such a songster he is sometimes known as the hedge accentor, but I think that is too grand a name for such a humble person. If you don't wish to think of him as a hedge-sparrow, you can call him a dunnock, and that probably suits him best. The wonderful thing about him is that though he is such a sober-coloured bird, with his dull brown back and grey head, his nest and eggs are among the loveliest of those of all our birds, and you should be able to find them in almost any

park or garden. To begin with, the nest, which is usually built low down in some bush or hedge in a pile of sticks or a hole in the wall, is a beautiful thing, cleverly made of mosses, lined snugly with horse-hair or wool. It is usually well hidden, and you would often miss it if it were not for the eggs. These are greeny-blue, and shine so in the nest that they catch your eye at once. It is difficult for me to tell you how lovely they are or describe the exact colour of the blue. I should say it is somewhere between sky-blue and Cambridge-blue, but the best plan will be for you to find a nest for yourself. You will soon manage this if you hunt about in March or April.

Now we come to two large families—the finches and tits. Only some of these will be familiar friends, most of them will be casual acquaintances, and a few so uncommon that we will only mention them by name. The finch family is probably the biggest bird family of all if we include all its near relations—the buntings, linnets, and redpolls. Many of these are quite common, but only two are what you would call everyday folk—the chaffinch and the greenfinch. It may surprise you, especially if your home is in a city or town, to know that the chaffinch is as common as the sparrow, and in some places more common. He doesn't look common at all. Indeed, the cock chaffinch is a distinguished looking gentleman, with his crested head of slatey-blue, his pinky breast, and chestnut-brown back. Even the hen is less drab than most hen birds, though, of course, she has none of the gay colours of her husband. There is another reason why you may at first find it hard to believe chaffinches are so common. You will not find their nests so often as you will those of blackbirds, thrushes, or hedge-sparrows. To begin with, it will be something of an event for you to find one, because they are usually so well hidden and camouflaged. The nest may be put in a hedge, on a branch or in the fork of a tree, and its nearly always beautifully made—a deep cup-shaped affair, made of soft mosses and wool, and lined with feathers, horse-hair, or down. But what makes it so difficult to see is the cunning way in which the outside is decorated with lichen, which exactly matches that growing on the tree or shrub in which the nest is built. Common the chaffinch may be, but his nest is one of the prettiest and most delicate of all our birds. Indeed, I would say that it is only beaten for beauty by those of the goldfinch, the goldcrest, and the long-tailed tit. The chaffinch's egg is distinctive. To tell you that it is bluey-white or dirty-white, with spots and blotches of deep reddy-brown—which look as if they have been put on with a brush while the egg was wet so that the colours have run—will not help you very much. A bird's egg is the most difficult thing to describe, and far the best way is to make up your mind you will see for yourself. But if you have a bird-table the chaffinch will be one of your first and most regular visitors, and will become friendly to the point of tameness quicker almost than any other bird. In springtime he has a cheerful little song and his confident cry of "Spink! Spink!" will greet you every day.

O.B.B   E

PARTRIDGES

Here's a little verse which I think sums up the chaffinch. It's called "The Dandy":

> "A sprightly bird is the chaffinch bold,
>   And in truth a beautiful thing,
> With his slate-blue crest, and rosy brest,
>   And the cream upon his wing.
> And his cheerful lay has melody
>   As he swings from an apple-tree,
> And the nest that is built by his dainty wife
>   Is the loveliest thing to see.
> ' Gay as a chaffinch,' say the French,
>   And they should surely know."

When I was a boy, the greenfinch was one of my father's garden enemies. He said it was destructive. I think now he gave it too bad a reputation, for although the greenfinch will and does regularly come into our parks and gardens to build his nest, he is not quite as close a friend of ours as are the other birds we have talked about. He is more a bird of the fields, the hedgerows, and the farmyard, and far more of a crowd-bird. He pines so much for company that he will often put his nest close to those of several other greenfinches, so that you may find quite a colony nesting together. His nest, by the way, is nothing like as pretty or as carefully made as the chaffinch, and the eggs are rather ordinary, being what you might call an off-white, with a few small reddy-brown spots. When you first notice him in winter you will probably think the greenfinch is rather ordinary looking too, and wonder why he should be called green. When you see him in his summer suit you will know. He is then an olive-green, shading off to lighter green, and when he flies you will be surprised at the flash of bright yellow-green from under his wings or tail.

Lastly, you will be certain to see at least two of the tit family—the great tit and the blue tit, and a cheeky couple they are too! By the way, the name tit is short for tit-mouse, which, I think, sounds far better, though there are other birds—for instance the wren or the tree-creeper—which we shall come to later on, which remind me more of a mouse. The tit-mice are a largish family. Besides the great tit-mouse and the blue tit-mouse, there are the coal tit-mouse, the marsh tit-mouse, and long-tailed tit-mouse, the bearded tit-mouse (which I told you, lives in the reed-beds not far from my home), the crested tit-mouse, and the rare willow tit-mouse. As you would guess from their names, the tit-mice are mostly tiny birds, all more or less highly coloured. The great tit-mouse is by far the biggest. He is sometimes called the oxeye and sometimes "saw-sharpener," because he has a funny, rasping little song —if you can call such a queer noise a song!—which sounds just like someone filing a saw-blade. He is handsome in a swaggering sort of way, with his

black head, white cheeks, and yellow tummy, but not nearly as beautiful as
the blue tit-mouse which, except that he also has a yellow tummy, is mostly a
lovely pale powder-blue. You cannot help noticing these two. They just force
their acquaintance on you by their cheekiness. They don't seem to be the least
bit afraid of us. They will be among the first arrivals at your bird-table, and
if they have found you have put out any food, they will quickly invite
all their friends. If you disturb them, they are quite likely to sit up on a
near-by branch and chatter and scold at you. In fact they are hot-tempered
little people, and I fancy that they are so busy getting angry that they have
no time to be afraid.

The blue tit has the nicer character of the two. He is certainly always ready
to swear or fight if put out by anything, but he is a most charming person to
watch, especially if, as I said, you feed him in winter with pieces of bacon or
cheese rind hung by a string. Within a short time two or three blue tit-mice
will arrive, talk excitedly to one another, and then probably perch on the
string and slide down it to the food. That does not satisfy them. They must
go underneath it and eat it from below, and don't they tuck in! You can easily
entice them indoors if you can bear to keep your windows open, and they are
even bold enough to venture into the house in spring-time to pick bits of fluff
or feathers for their nests. They build these nests in holes in old trees, walls,
buildings, or spouts. They don't seem to bother where the hole is so long as
it is narrow and fairly deep, so that inquisitive people cannot reach it with their
fingers. If you want to see how unafraid a tit really is, you have only to
find a nest with a mother tit-mouse sitting on her eggs. Does she fly off when
you try and reach it with your fingers? Not she. Of course she couldn't
really, because your hand will be blocking up the hole. The point is, she doesn't
try, nor does she cringe away. She just chatters angrily and tries her best to
peck you. If you think of it, you will see how comical, though brave, it is for
such a tiny scrap of a bird to attack a great big thing like yourself. The nest
is a comfortable snuggery made of lots of feathers and moss, and the eggs of
both these tit-mice, great and blue, are white with small brown spots. There
will usually be quite a lot of them, from six to nine. Sometimes other birds
like sparrows will try to pinch the hole for their own nests, or to push the
tits away from the food you have thrown out. They rarely succeed, for the
tits rush at them with such boldness that Philip Sparrow and his friends,
though bigger and stronger, will usually think better of it.

The only small bird that the blue tit-mouse seems to fear is his great tit-
mouse cousin, and I am afraid that that gentleman is more than a bit of a
bully and a robber. He looks the part, I think. What I particularly dislike
about him is his nasty habit of eating honey-bees. Each year, when the first
spring warmth strikes the hives, the bees, weak after their long winter sleep,
crawl out to stretch their wings in the sun. That is the moment the great
tit-mice will be waiting for, and they will pounce down on the poor bees, and

gobble them up. And if the bees are still keeping to the shelter of their hives, the birds will come down and tap on the alighting boards with their beaks. Out come the bees to see who is knocking, and, of course, are caught and eaten one by one. So at that time of the year I always keep watch on my bee-hives with a gun, and bang off at the robbers, mostly to frighten them, though sometimes I have to kill two or three before they will stop. It may be that you will also see the coal-tit with the other two. He is about the same size as the blue-tit, though he is altogether a darker bird. Also he is not so common or quite so cheeky. Otherwise his habits are much the same.

There are other birds, of course, which you may think of as familiar friends. If you live at the seaside, for example, or even in London, the seagull may be one. If you live in the country, the rook and the wild pigeon will be others. But I don't think they are quite the same as those I have told you about, because they will not be close to you and your homes in the same companionable way. You may well ask why I have not mentioned birds like the swallows and the house-martins, for example. The answer is, of course, that these and many other birds are only with us for a few months in the year. These are the visitors which pay us the compliment of coming all the way from wild, hot parts of Africa to build their nests in our gardens, our parks and woods, and to bring off their families in Britain where people—all decent people, that is—are kind to birds and love them. I shall have lots to say about them later when we talk about " Visitors."

THE BIRDTABLE

Chapter III

ACQUAINTANCES OF THE FIELDS

IF we wish to widen the circle of our friends and make fresh ones, we shall generally have to seek them outside our parks and gardens, in the fields and woods, along river-banks or on the seashore. That does not mean that we may not see many more birds in our town parks or country garden than those we have just talked about. We shall—so long as we keep our eyes open, for you will never see much if you go about with them half-shut. All kinds of birds will wander into big cities. I have watched a great, long-legged heron— our British stork—sailing about in the sky over Victoria Station in London, looking for a spot beside the lake in the grounds of Buckingham Palace where he could do a little quiet fishing, or catch a few royal frogs. Before he flew down he settled in a tall tree and stayed there a few minutes, looking all round to see if the coast was clear. It was odd to see such a wild sort of bird perched above the traffic of a busy London street. I have had a nuthatch—a very pretty, friendly bird—on a bird-table in North London, and a fly-catcher nesting in the creeper just below my bedroom window within sound of the buses. And even if your home is bang in the middle of a big city, you are almost sure to hear an owl hooting or squeaking round it at night. So you can never be certain what birds you may see anywhere. Still, as I told you at the beginning, the birds which you are likely to see in one part of Britain may be very unlikely arrivals in another part. Some of them will never be seen in some districts and yet be common in others. For instance, if you live in Scotland or Northern England you will have little difficulty in seeing grouse, but they are birds which never live in the southern counties of England. Then there are birds like the bearded tit-mouse which we have already mentioned, which are only to be found in one district in all the British Isles—that is, in Norfolk and parts of Suffolk.

Suppose we make a start with the birds of field and woodland, and begin where we left off with the other members of the finch and tit-mouse families.

HAWFINCH

The finches first. Many of the finches are likely at some time or another to venture near our homes, especially in winter, when times are hard and birds go hungry. The bullfinch certainly. He will go almost anywhere in search of food. He is a very hungry person. Indeed, you won't be far wrong if you call him greedy. He will eat almost till he bursts. If you know a privet hedge, keep a watch on it when it is covered with its little black berries and you may catch sight of the bullfinches having a real bullfinch blow-out. They simply stuff themselves, and fly off, looking as if their wings could scarcely carry their tummies away! In Suffolk the bullfinch is called the "olph-bird." Why, I cannot tell you, but somehow the name suits him. He is such a jolly, sturdy person, and his suit is so richly coloured. His head looks as if someone had crammed a black skull-cap too far down on it, and his thick, short beak gives the impression that he is always puffing for breath. But look at his lovely crimson chest, his blue-grey coat, and the splodge of white where his black tail joins his back. There is no other finch with so distinctive a uniform. The hen bullfinch is very like her mate, with the same black skull-cap, but, of course, her colours are less bright, and where he is crimson she is brown. The bullfinches range all over Britain, and their nest is a rougher, stronger copy of the greenfinches. The eggs are bluish, with little purple and black spots. The bullfinch is one of my particular favourites. If you keep one in a cage he will soon become very tame, and when I was a boy I had one which would eat seeds from between my lips, and even sit on a toy trumpet while I blew it. He used to be out of his cage all the time we were in the room, and was only put into it when we went out, to save him from the cat. He lived to be many years old before he died of over-eating. Bull-finches whistle rather than sing, and have even been taught to talk a little. When you have learnt their short whistling call you will hear it often when you cannot see the birds, and if you make it they will answer you.

Partly, I expect, because I am so fond of him, I think the bullfinch is the handsomest of the finches, but you will probably present the beauty prize to the goldfinch. He is a little smaller than the bullfinch or greenfinch, and built on more delicate lines. There is no doubt he is a most gaily-coloured bird, so gaily-coloured in fact, that he looks almost foreign. I like to think of him as a bird of the sun, and he is a flash of sunshine as he flits across gorse or cornfields to alight on a thistlehead, light almost as thistledown himself. And what a splash of colour he makes, with his red and gold against the purple of the thistle! Thistle seeds are his favourite food, and though he often comes into orchards and gardens to make his nest, he is a shy person, and is seldom tempted into the cold north country. In some parts of England he is known as the "King Harry." His nest is the most beautiful thing, softer and more delicate even than that of the chaffinch. You may often find it on the gnarled, lichen-covered branch of an old fruit-tree in the orchard. The eggs are like those of the greenfinch, only smaller.

Before we leave the finches, we ought to mention the hawfinch and the crossbill—the hawfinch, because he is by far the biggest finch, and the crossbill because he is such an unusual person. Neither of them are birds you are likely to see just anywhere—in fact you will be rather lucky to see either of them. If you look at the picture of the hawfinch you may well say size is not everything, and think he is a clumsy, lumpy looking bird, with his big head, heavy blue beak, and short tail. He looks all out of proportion, doesn't he? But he is a terror in the garden, and the damage he can do to your fruit or peas will explain why his beak is so big and strong. He can crack the stones of damsons and sloes with it quite easily. The crossbill gets his name because of his beak, which, as you will see, has the bottom part crossed over the top one. It is really a powerful pair of snippers, so that he can snip off pine-cones and eat the seeds inside them. Crossbills live on pine-seeds, and are only found in districts where there are lots of pine-trees, specially in Scotland and in Eastern England. They live together in colonies, making their nests—which are much like those of the bullfinch or greenfinch—high up in the branches of the pines. If you stand under the trees in which they are nesting, you may see showers of pieces of cone fluttering down as the birds are feeding. The funny thing about the crossbill, apart from his specially shaped bill, is that he often begins to nest as early in the year as January—that is, in mid-winter; and, as you may imagine, snow and rain ruin many a crossbill home. So the birds may make another attempt in summer as late as June and July. No other bird is quite so peculiar in its habits, except perhaps the wood-pigeon, which has been found nesting all the year round from early March to November. I always remember the first time I saw a crossbill. I was just being lazy, which is a very good thing to be sometimes if you want to watch birds, and was lying in the sunshine near a sort of dew-pond in a Norfolk pine-wood. All sorts of ordinary folk, like robins, chaffinches, hedge-sparrows and blackbirds, had been down to drink and bath, when there suddenly appeared a bird which, with the sunlight on his feathers, looked blood-red. I knew he was a crossbill, because I remembered the old legend which tells how he got his crossed beak and crimson coat. At the Crucifixion, the crossbill, it is said, lighted on the cross on which Our Lord was hanging, and, moved with pity, tried to help by pulling out the nails which held Him there. Of course they were hammered in far too hard for even his strong beak, but as he tugged, his beak became crossed, and his feathers stained with the blood of Jesus. I cannot help thinking of the crossbill as a kind of small, red parrot. Besides his beak, which is something like a parrot's, he has a trick of pulling himself from branch to branch by it which is also what a parrot does.

Two other dainty little cousins of the finches are the linnet and the redpoll. Now you may hear people talking about a green linnet, a grey linnet, a brown linnet, and a red linnet. You can tell them they are wrong. What they call the green linnet is only the greenfinch by another name, and the others are all the same bird, which is just—the linnet. There is only one linnet, and the reason he is called grey, brown, or red is simply because in winter the hen linnet is greyish and her husband brown, while in summer he is a rather splendid person, with a crimson chest and forehead. They are not garden birds, and much prefer downland or commons, all the wild scrubby places which are not ploughed or cared for by farmers. You will usually find the linnet's nest in a gorse bush or a low hedge. It is quite a pretty one, being built of twig and grass, and lined with wool, hair, and feathers and thistledown. Its eggs are much the same as those of most of the finches—a sort of faintly-bluish white, with little browny-purple spots and streaks at the big end. The linnet used to be very popular as a cage bird, and in the busy towns of Yorkshire and Durham and in London lots of people would keep them in little cages. This was to make them sing, and their owners would hold linnet-singing competitions to see who had the best songster. Of course, it was not pleasant to see a bird penned up in a cage where there was barely room for it to stretch its wings, much less to fly. But I often wonder whether caged birds are really as miserable as people say they are, provided that the cages are big and roomy enough. Not many years ago my father took a nest of young linnets while the birds were still tiny. He did not move the nest away, but put it inside a big cage so that the parent birds could come and feed the young ones through the bars. They did this till the young ones were old enough to feed themselves from a tin of bird-seed put into the cage. They were not very old when one day my father took them out into the garden to get some sunshine, and someone accidentally opened the door of the cage. Away went all the young

PHEASANTS

CROSSBILL

linnets. No doubt they were glad to be free and to use their wings as Nature meant them to do. The interesting fact is, that when next day my father was feeding his hens, he noticed two or three small birds fluttering about close-by. They were his escaped linnets! He ran and fetched the cage, put some seed inside, and left the door open. Within a few minutes four of the missing five youngsters had gone back to the cage, and there they lived a long and seemingly happy life.

The redpoll is not unlike the linnet. Indeed, if you were just to catch sight of one in the distance you would probably say it was a linnet. The chief difference is the patch of red on his head. It is from this that he gets his name, for poll is an old English name for head. It is not so common as the linnet, though it may be found almost anywhere, particularly in the North Country. The redpoll also used to be popular as a cage-bird. For one thing, it is so little afraid of you and me that it can easily be caught ; and for another, it soon becomes tame and can be taught to do little tricks, like ringing a bell when it is hungry or pulling up its seeds in a thimble tied to the end of a thread of cotton. Both the nest and eggs are also very similar to the linnet's, and the best way to know one from t'other is to learn to recognise the birds and their songs. Those of you who live in Northern England and Scotland may see a close relation of the linnets—the twite. Indeed, he is often called a mountain linnet, because he likes high wild places and makes his nest in the heather.

The other day a man said to me: "Can you tell me the name of a yellow bird which lives in Cornwall? It is like a canary, and it seems to like hedgerows." Now fancy anyone not knowing that the bird he had seen was the common yellow-hammer, or yellow-bunting, which lives not only in Cornwall but

LINNET

almost anywhere in the British Isles. It does live in hedges, and that is why you will probably see it first, and oftenest, as you walk along a country road. You cannot mistake it. The hen bird is not very yellow, but her husband's head is as bright a yellow as a canary's, and his tummy too, is a fairly bright yellow. You will see him sitting in the road or on top of a hedge, and the pity is that now farmers are cutting down their hedges they are turning the yellow-hammers, as well as many another bird, out of house and home. One day they will be sorry for this, I fancy, because the yellow-hammer eats many of the insects which destroy crops. He is a nice person, though you could never say he was a friendly bird. He prefers the roadside hedge to our gardens, and builds his nest very low down, often on the ground at the bottom of the hedge or on the bank between hedge and ditch. It's an ordinary kind of nest, built of grass and hair, but the eggs are quite out of the ordinary. They are a sort of dirty white, but covered with dark lines and squiggles, which look for all the world as if someone had taken a pen and scribbled over them. Indeed, in some parts the yellow-hammer is called the "writing lark" or "scribbling lark," because of his funnily marked eggs. If you have a quick ear for music you will soon pick out his song. I was always told as a boy that he sang a "little bit of bread and *no* cheese!" The yellow-hammer is the commonest of the large family of buntings which are close relations of the finches. The only other common bunting which you are likely to see more or less anywhere is the corn-bunting, but he is such an ordinary looking person that you do not easily spot him. Except that he has no bright colours, he is much the same as his yellow cousin. The reed-bunting is also fairly common, but he isn't a field-dweller. As you can tell from his name,

he lives in marshy places or on river-banks among the reeds. Still, we ought to mention him here with his relations, especially since, on account of his dark head and throat with its white collar, he is easy to spot. There are many other buntings, but I don't think we will bother about them here.

Now for the tit-mice. You will remember we have already talked about the great, the blue, and the coal tit-mouse. There are many others, but the only two I am going to tell you about are the long-tailed tit-mouse and our old friend the bearded tit-mouse. The long-tailed tit is one of our most lovable little birds. He is to be found almost all over our country (except in the very North of Scotland), though you are most likely to notice him in winter when he flits about in happy family parties from tree to tree and bush to bush. His wings are so short that he cannot make long flights, and as he flies, his tail is held out straight behind him to act as a rudder and a balance. He is a beautiful pinky person, and he is also just about our champion nest-builder. It is because of his nest that he is sometimes called the "bottle-tit" or "feather-poke." When you have been lucky enough to find his nest you will know why. I cannot tell you where to look for this wonderful piece of bird home-building, because it is put in all sorts of places—I have found it in a gorze bush, in a bush, a hedge, and in a tree. But when you have found it you will know at once. To begin with, it is a domed nest, something like the wren's, only bigger and deeper, and much more beautifully made. In it, wool and moss and lichens are woven together with the silken threads of spider's web, and the outside camouflaged with lichen and bits of moss to make it difficult to see. Inside it is filled with hundreds upon hundreds of feathers. As many as 2,000 have been counted in one nest. Altogether it is a most cosy and water-proof house. The most extraordinary thing is that in this bottle-shaped ball Mrs. Long-tailed Tit lays as many as twelve eggs or more. What you will wonder is how she manages to get her long tail into it. The answer is that she bends it back over her head, so that the tip of her tail and her head fill up the entrance hole to the nest like a cork in a bottle. Not a drop of rain or breath of air can get in. Just think of the squash and the fug when there are ten or twelve young tit-mice in it besides mother! And to make the crowding worse, father may push in somehow to keep warm too! I wonder they do not all suffocate. The truth is, that these long-tails feel the cold dreadfully, and a hard winter often kills them off in large numbers. Unfortunately, we can do nothing to help by putting out food for them, because they are insect-eaters.

The bearded tit-mouse or reedling—because he isn't a true tit-mouse, only a close relation—should not come into this book by rights, because he is a very rare gentleman, whom you are only likely to see if you live near or happen to visit the Norfolk Broads. Still, we have already mentioned him, and he is so comical, with his drooping black whiskers, that I had to put him in. Also, he is a good example of a bird which has been saved for us by people

WOOD PIGEON

YELLOW-HAMMER

taking care of him. His home is in the reed-beds of wild marshy places—his feathers are the colour of old reeds—but as our towns spread into the country and more land is wanted for houses or for farmers to grow our food, the marshes have to be drained and turned into fields. So it comes about that there are fewer and fewer places where the bearded tit-mouse can live. Not so long ago they had nearly all gone, and only a few birds were left. Then wise men took care to see that nice reed-beds were set aside for them to nest in, and no one was allowed to take their eggs. Now there are again quite a lot of these whiskery little marsh people—if you know where to look for them—and that is all to the good.

Two small birds that you are almost sure to see every time you take a walk through country fields are the lark and the tit-lark. They will rise out of the grass or the stubbles at your feet. Both are alike in one thing—they make their nests on the ground. The lark either finds a shallow hole in field or meadow or scoops one out for himself and lines it with dried grasses. The tit-lark is a little more painstaking. His nest, which is stuck under a tussock or in rough grass, or maybe in the heather—because he likes the moorlands— is also made of grass, but is usually lined with horse-hair. Even the eggs are not unlike. Both are browny to match the earth. The lark's egg is a grey, which is so covered with dirty brown spots that you can hardly see any white. The tit-lark's is a bit smaller, and more of a reddy-brown. When you think how easy it is for prowling cat or hunting weasel, rat or mouse to find these nests, or even for them to be trodden on by the clumsy great hooves of cows and horses, not to mention your feet, you will wonder

SKYLARK

how it is that each year the larks and tit-larks bring off so many of their young ones. For both these birds are plentiful almost anywhere we like to go. Except that they are both ground-dwellers of our fields, the two birds have nothing in common. They are not related and their habits are different. The skylark, to give him his proper name, belongs to the lark family, although it has only one cousin, the woodlark, which also nests in Great Britain. The tit-lark you should know as the meadow-pipit, and the pipits are relatives of the wag-tails, which we shall come to later on. The skylark is, of course, one of our famous singers. Most of you know the poem "Hark, hark, the lark at Heaven's Gate sings." That is just about what he does. To say that he sings as he flies is not the whole story. What he does is to rise from the ground and climb steeply up into the sky, beating his way heavenwards with quivering wings, and as he mounts he fairly shouts his song. When he is no more than a speck against the blue, he will swing round in a circle and then glide swiftly down again, still singing. He is up long before daylight in summer, ready to greet the sun in the dawn chorus, and he will sing all day.

Even on sunny days in winter he will pour his song out on the earth below. The curious thing about his song is that it is beautiful when heard at a distance, but rather loud and shrieky when you hear it close to you. We once had a tame lark which lived in a big cage which we called its hotel, and in which we used to put fresh sods cut from the meadow. When that bird burst into song it filled the room with so much sound that it almost deafened us. The meadow-pipit is not anything like as good a flyer, and hasn't anything like the same song. It will flutter up from the grass or heather, and down again, and it does sing as it flies, but you could not really call it a songster. The meadow-pipit has two cousins which nest with us. One of these, the rock-pipit, is a seashore bird, and the other, the tree-pipit, which is found more in woodlands, is one of our summer visitors. All are browny birds, and you will find it difficult to tell one from the other. Both make their nests on or near the ground, the tree-pipit usually under a tree in old bracken or coarse grass, and the rock-pipit on a bank, in a cleft in the rocks or on the ground. The peculiar thing about the tree-pipit is that it lays different coloured eggs. They may be quite pale ones, mottled with darkish brown, or else browny or reddish, covered with red or purple markings like marble. The purple kind are really beautiful, and not like those of any other of our birds.

Before you notice the pipits you are almost sure to have spotted the wagtails. There are a number of them which are to be seen in Britain, but only two—the pied-wagtail and the grey-wagtail—live with us all the year, though the yellow wagtail is a visitor who nests in parts of England and Scotland. The one you will know best is the pied wagtail. It is often called the water-wagtail, but this name is really better earned by its grey cousin, for although the pied one likes to dabble about in water after insects, it is the grey one which lives near water. Altogether these wagtail names are a bit of a puzzle, because the grey-wagtail is almost as yellow a bird as the one which is called yellow! The one name which does fit them is wagtail. As they walk or run along the ground, they keep on wagging their long tails up and down. The pied-wagtail is much the commonest, and likes especially to come close to our houses or farms. Indeed, he often seems to be showing himself off, though he has no need to draw attention to himself with such a startling black and white livery. You simply cannot miss him because of his black head and back, white chest and tummy and white face, which also reminds me somehow of a clown at the circus. Garden lawns, especially after they have been mown, are a favourite place for him to run about on, but he is just as fond of farmyards and ploughland. Of course he is after the grubs, insects and things on which he feeds, and if you watch him you will see that every now and then he hops into the air to snatch at a fly. He is an attractive person, with little fear of you and me, always on the go, but never seeming to be in a hurry. I just cannot tell you where best to look for his nest. He puts it in all sorts of places. I have found it in haystacks and in the creepers against the wall of a house, and in an old wall, but it may be built on the ground or even in the old nest of some other bird. It is mostly a grass and leaf affair, lined with hair and wool, and sometimes with feathers. In it the hen wagtail lays four to six eggs, usually of a dirty white colour speckled with greyish spots and often streaked with fine lines. The pied-wagtail can be seen almost any-where. Not so the grey one. He is much less a common acquaintance. While the pied-wagtail haunts our gardens as well as our fields, the grey one sticks close to water, and especially to the quick-running rivers and rills of hilly

GREAT SPOTTED WOODPECKER

GREEN WOODPECKER

MEADOW-PIPIT

country, which, as you can imagine, are generally far from our daily haunts. This wagtail has a slate-grey head and back, but his underparts are a bright yellow. I am sure that when you see him you will call him yellow rather than grey. He makes the same sort of nest as his pied cousin, but puts it in a crevice in the rocks or wall or bank, and nearly always near running water. The yellow-wagtail is not only a visitor—he is too uncommon to be put amongst our ordinary acquaintances.

All the birds we have so far talked about are what are known as passeres, a Latin word which means perchers—that is, birds which perch on something, a branch or a tussock of grass, or hop along the ground. Now we must take a look at a bird—the plover—which belongs to the waders, those which walk or run along the ground, particularly in water or marshland. Most of these we shall come to when we talk about the birds of river, lake, and shore, but I think we ought to deal with the plover now, because he is truly a bird of our fields. Whether your home is in a county of grassland and heather, or among the fat corn-lands of the south, you are sure to see the plover, though he always prefers to be somewhere near water, like a lot of boys and girls I know. He visits the mudbanks at the mouths of rivers or wild marshland to find nice juicy worms and snails, but in spring he usually comes inland to our meadows and cornfields or moorland pastures to lay his eggs and bring up his young ones. As he is a walking instead of a hopping bird, his babies are born with big feet. The mother bird has a good idea that if she lets them get too near wet clay or mud they are likely to get their feet so clogged up with it that they will not be able to walk, and may easily die. Anyway, you can hardly miss the plover. I can imagine you first seeing a crowd of birds standing or running

PIED-WAGTAIL

about on a mud-flat or in a field. As you get close you will see that what at a distance looked like a blackish bird is really a most handsome and distinguished person. What will strike you, I am sure, is his lovely shape, with his wings folded sleekly on his back and his black crest standing up behind his head. You will notice the gentle brown eye set in his white cheek, his black collar and pinky legs, one of them usually poised off the ground as if he were not sure whether to take a step forward or fly away. He has seen you, you may be sure. What he is not sure about is whether you are a friend or an enemy. As he moves, you will suddenly see that what looked like a black back is really a rich greenish-bronze, with a purple sheen on his shoulder feathers. As the sun strikes it, it glows with colour. Then, when with two or three quick flaps of his broad, rounded wings he floats into the air, you will again be surprised at the rich chestnut colouring under his tail. He always goes about in large crowds. He even nests in colonies, on the ground of course, though you can hardly call his a nest. Indeed, he makes no pretence at building anything, and is quite content to find a convenient spot in grass or ploughland, where the hen will lay four eggs—lovely olive-green ones, with dark-brown splodges which almost exactly match the colour of the earth. It is marvellous to think how eggs open to a host of dangers hatch out so often, especially when by nesting so many in one place, the plovers almost invite animals or people to find them. Plover's eggs are good to eat, and at one time were taken in such numbers to sell as food that there was a danger that the birds would die out. That would have been a calamity, because the plover is not only beautiful but one of our more useful birds, eating many insects or worms which harm the farmer's crops, so a law was made saying you must not take their eggs. Thanks to that law there are to-day lots of plovers again, as you will see. The eggs are very fat at one end and pointed at the other. You will always find them arranged with the pointed ends towards the centre. However many times you alter the arrangement, the patient bird will turn them back again. So far I have used the name plover, but he has others you may know better—

lapwing, for example, or pee-wit or peese-wheep. As soon as you have come to know him you will understand the reason for the last two. They are as nearly as possible the sound of his cry. "Pee-ee-wit! Wit! Wit! Pee-ee-wit!" It is a queer, plaintive little cry, and as he utters it he will be tumbling over and over in the sky, now falling towards the ground, then banking steeply, somersaulting again, and then flapping slowly for a second or two. He is a bit of an acrobat is the plover, and more than a bit of an actor too, as you will see if you start to try and find his nest. To begin with, all the plovers nesting in the field in which you are searching will rise into the air with loud cries. Then it is rather like a game of hunt-the-thimble, except that, when you get "hot," the cock bird will try and distract you by flying so close that he almost hits your head, while the hen may alight and try to lead you away from her nest by pretending she has a wounded wing, which she will drag behind her! I have sat hours in a field watching the antics of nesting plovers, and I imagine some of you will one day do the same, for the plover is a really fascinating personality. He has a lot of relations which visit us in summer—the golden plover (he is not really golden, only yellow flecked, and not so handsome as the green plover in spite of his proud name), the grey plover, and the Kentish plover, for example—but only one which stays with us all the year round, the ringed plover, and he is definitely a seaside bird, whom we shall come to later.

The curlew, like the plover, is a shore bird in winter and an inland bird in spring and summer. I should not, perhaps, put him among the field acquaintances we are likely to make, but I do so because to those of you who live in or near moorland country he will be as familiar a person as the plover to those of you who live in or visit the lowlands. He is a big bird, nearly as big as a domestic fowl, but I always link him in my mind with the plover, although he is no close relation. He is a wader, and nests on the ground. He has something of the same sort of cry as the plover, only it is weirder and more varied. Sometimes in winter he will just call something which sounds like "Koor-lee," but in spring and summer you may recognise him from his sharp cry of "Whaup"—from which he gets his Scottish name of whaup—or the longer "Koor-lyou," from which comes his English name of curlew. The last is a most mournful wail, which I always remember from my boyhood the birds would make at dusk as they flew from one side of the valley in which we lived to the other. There is another curious bubbly sort of call they sometimes utter, which is rather pleasant when you know what it is, though it may startle you at first. He is a comical-looking bird, soberly dressed in a suit of grey. His peculiarity, of course, is his beak—a long, downward curving thing, something like a trunk. Indeed, an old grey curlew standing up in the heather always puts me in mind of an elephant. He is supposed to be very wise, and is certainly very brave, as you will find if you go close to its eggs. The curlew is little more of a nest-builder than a plover, and it lays either on the

MAGPIE

JAY

moors, where the heather is not too deep, or in the fields on the moor's edge. Its eggs are not unlike those of the plover, though they are not so dark in shade, and, of course, much bigger.

To end the list of common acquaintances of the fields let's turn to the game birds—particularly the partridge, the pheasant, and their cousin the grouse. All are ground-dwellers and nesters like the plovers and curlew, but they are runners rather than waders. Runners don't usually choose swampy ground over which to show their speed, but pheasants and grouse both like to keep near marshy places, because these give them plenty of food and are nice and cool in hot weather. The pheasant, indeed, is not even afraid to swim if need be. When we call them game birds we mean that they are fair game to shoot because they are good to eat. Also, when they do fly, they fly fast, for which reason many people find it exciting to shoot at them. It is not at all easy to hit a partridge or a high pheasant or a grouse as it comes whirring over the heather. You have to be a good shot, so that shooting these birds is a game of skill. Even if you have to live in towns, you will have seen all of them at some time or another for sale in the game-dealers, or fishmongers' shops, though however much you like roast pheasant or grouse pie, you will scarcely recognise these scraps of battered feathers hanging limply on hooks as the same birds you can see alive and lovely in the country.

Strictly speaking, only the partridge is a true field bird, but I think game birds are best placed among our field acquaintances, because your first sight of a live pheasant is more likely to be when he is feeding on the stubbles in autumn than in the woods where he lives; and because the grouse is, as I have already said, a bird of the moorlands, which are open spaces. What you must remember about all game birds is that they are protected people, who are not allowed to lead quite natural lives. Since they provide both good sport and good food, we want to have lots more of them than could survive naturally, so we protect them from their enemies, and also see that there is enough food for these large numbers of birds to eat. You can only shoot them during certain months of the year, though all year round the gamekeepers and others are shooting or trapping the animals or birds which prey upon them. There are even game farms, where partridges and pheasants are bred, and the eggs hatched off by hens or bantams.

The partridge is a popular person, as well he may be. He is a bird of the farmlands. Not for him any wind-swept heath or tangled wood. He sticks as close to the farmer as he can, because he knows that there he need never go short of food, so long as he keeps to the corn and root fields, and summons enough courage to venture into a stackyard in winter. He is rather delicate, so that it is probably as well he is protected; but he looks so plump and contented that I imagine he does himself pretty well. You are first likely to see partridges crouching in a field. At a distance they look like clods of earth, and when they begin to move they seem to creep like beetles. Then an old cock

CURLEW

will stick up his head, and you will notice that, though the partridge's full name is the common or grey partridge, he is far more than grey. His chest and tummy are grey, it is true, but on them is a chocolate-red mark shaped like a horseshoe. His head is a sort of chestnut brown and his back is brown. The partridge makes its nest in the bottom of a hedge or in some longish grass. It is not much of an affair as nests go, and in it you may find anything from ten to fifteen eggs! These are nice shiny olive brown all over—you could almost call them khaki. Most of these eggs will hatch out, but, of course, not all the "cheepers" grow up. Suppose from seven to twelve young "cheepers" survive to join father and mother, they all go about in autumn and winter in a family party called a "covey." Partridges are family birds, and father and mother partridge make a very loving and faithful pair of parents. Partridges mate once and for life. That means that if the hen partridge get herself killed by a weasel or a cat, or even run over on the road by a motor-car, the cock bird is such a good father that he will take over all the family duties and look after his brood until they are grown up and able to fend for themselves. He will never seek another wife.

The common partridge is a truly British bird, even if he may owe his numbers to the protection he is given. You cannot say that about the rather flashy bird which is known as the red-legged or French partridge. This bird was only brought into England from Europe not much more than a hundred years ago, and is not properly a partridge, but what is known as a chuckor. He is not to be found all through the country like the common partridge, and has settled chiefly in the eastern and southern parts of England. He's a bigger and more aggressive-looking person than our own little grey bird, and it used to be thought that he drove the grey partridge away from the

RED-LEGGED PARTRIDGE

districts where he lived. This isn't true, and actually the Englishman is the
boss of the two, but because of it, and because the Frenchman is not so exciting
to shoot at, he is not protected like the other game birds. In fact, he is treated
rather roughly, which is perhaps a pity, because he's an interesting and gaily
coloured bird. The French partridge builds much the same kind of nest in
much the same sort of places as the common partridge, but its eggs—of which
you may find from eight to twelve or more—are of a sandy colour, speckled
with darkish red spots.

Even if you have not seen him swaggering about in all his glory, the
pheasant is unmistakable. Both he and his wife have long tails, unlike most
other British birds. Also, although the hen is quietly dressed like all hen
birds, the cock pheasant fairly blazes with colour, and in spring has two little
tufts like ears on his head. As you see him picking over the cornfields after
harvest or hunting about among the spring wheat, the sun shining on his
feathers sets them ablaze with rich colour. You may think that he looks far
less like a British bird even than the French partridge, and you will be right.
The first pheasants were brought to England hundreds of years ago by the
Romans. They come from Eastern Europe, and are known as the English
black-necks. Many others have since been brought in from India and China.
Though they have lived here ever since, they have never been able to get along
without help. In a sense the pheasant is the most coddled of our game birds—
that is to say, we try to keep hundreds of thousands more birds than could
ever keep themselves. They are spoon-fed people. Large numbers of
them are reared in farms and then turned out; but though they run about
in the woods and fields, they are not true wild birds, and certainly the hen

birds are not the good mothers that they should be. All too often Mrs. Pheasant does not show much loving care in making a comfy nest and being ready to defend her eggs or young ones. Indeed, she is so casual that she may often lay her eggs in another pheasant's nest. I have seen nests in which there were as many as forty eggs, which meant that three or four birds were laying in it. I expect she knows that her eggs are so precious that someone will be sure to come along and give them to some broody old barnyard fowl to sit on. In the ordinary way she lays from ten to a dozen eggs, bigger than those of the partridge, but a little richer in colour, usually in thickets of nettles and brambles in a wood. In the spring, when the pheasants are nesting, you may often hear from the depths of a wood a noise very much like the whistle of a railway engine. That will be the cock pheasant crowing with pride or rage as he challenges some other pheasant to a fight for a wife. Sometimes you may see him strutting round with the poultry in a farmyard, and altogether he has something of the same manners as an ordinary domestic cockrel. But that's not surprising, because he is a not very distant relative.

Lastly, there is the grouse—the red grouse. Like the partridge he is truly British. Indeed, he is found nowhere else in the world except Scotland, Wales, the North of Ireland, and the North of England. Also he is the least coddled of our game birds. That does not mean he is not protected at all. He is. The many enemies of the moorland which might attack him are shot, and each year wide tracts of heather are burnt so that next spring it will again grow in the tiny green shoots that the grouse loves. But he is a sturdy bird, and, because he keeps to the wild places, we cannot do so much for him as for partridges and pheasants which stick to the farmlands. The grouse is another of my favourites. Those of you who are lucky enough to come to know him will, I fancy, agree with me. As you trudge knee-deep through the heather, there will be a wild whirring at your feet, like a clockwork spring suddenly unwound. You may get a start, but it will only be a cock grouse you have almost trodden on. Away he will go, just above the heather, making a comic noise, for all the world like an old man chuckling "Kuk! Kuk! Kuk!" Then he will glide back into the heather, and shout something at you which sounds as if he were telling you to "Go-back! Go-back! Go-back-back-back!" When you are wise to his habits you may be able to get close enough to him to see the red wattles, as they are called, round and above his eyes, and his greyish, feathery trousers. His nest will take some finding. It will be no more than a grass-and-heather-lined hole beneath the heather, and in it the eight to twelve or more eggs, mottled all over with rich chocolate markings, will exactly match their surroundings. Sometimes there are heavy snowstorms high up on the hills while the hen grouse is sitting on her eggs. She takes no notice, and often goes on sitting though completely buried in the snow! The red grouse is an ancient Briton, but, as I have said, you need not expect to see him if your home is in the Midlands or the South of England. He has three relations—the black grouse, the capercaillie, and the ptarmigan, which, by the way, you pronounce as if it were spelt tarmigan without the p. But all these are birds of Scotland, and are so uncommon that we must not list them among the daily acquaintances of our fields and open spaces.

RED GROUSE

Chapter IV

ACQUAINTANCES OF TREES AND WOODS

YOU may find it will take you longer to get friendly with the birds of trees and woods. But that isn't surprising. The first birds we know will naturally be those at our back doors, and the next those which we see in our country walks, in hedges and fields, and on moor or common. The birds which live in trees or woods mostly have a reason—they wish to keep themselves to themselves, and try to do this either by nesting high up in a tall tree where they think they are out of reach, or deep in the wild wood where we cannot find them. The rooks, for example, take no trouble to hide their nests. As I have already told you, they seem to like placing their rookeries in a copse or spinney close to our houses, and besides their nests being great, ugly bundles of twigs and sticks, they make such a to-do when they are building them that you cannot help knowing where they are. But the nests are fixed to the thin branches in the tree-tops, and it is not very likely that any animal, let alone you and I, will venture to climb up to them. Lots of birds which nest in woods are summer visitors, but I don't want to talk about them now. Remember, we are still concerned only with the birds which stay in Britain all the year round. I want to keep the visitors by themselves, so that when we come to them you will get a good idea of how many of them there are.

There is another thing about woods. The thicker the trees or the bigger the wood the fewer small birds you are likely to find. That, I fancy, is because the little people know that such dark and gloomy places are the haunts of the robbers and killers, of the savage birds which go there so as to get away from the likes of you and me: jays, for example, which steal eggs, and the hawks and owls which live by killing and eating small animals and other birds. You can test this for yourselves. In the open sort of wood where grow trees like oak and ash and thorn, and where there are plenty of small bushes, bracken and brambles, you will find quite a lot of little birds, especially on the wood's fringe, where it meets the fields. Then see how many you will find in one of

55

those dark woods of fir and pine, where the trees are so close together you cannot see the sky, and there is no undergrowth but only a thick carpet of pine-needles. These are silent places, where you will seldom hear the sound of bird-song. They are the castles of the bandits of the bird-world, which prey on their smaller fellows, and I am sorry to say that the happy, open sort of wood, noisy with the singing and talking of birds, is becoming scarcer and scarcer, while the other sort is growing more common.

Yet fir-woods often shelter the smallest of all our birds—the gold-crest, or, as he is often called, the golden-crested wren. He is a real "tiddy-wee," the tiniest scrap of a thing. Look at him. His suit is just an ordinary khaki, but the crest on his head makes him look as if he was wearing one of our soldier's forage-caps—black on the outside and bright orange in the middle. He is a particularly busy person, hunting about the trees for insects and sometimes having to hang himself upside down like a tit-mouse to make a closer inspection of some branch or twig. You may not have to go into the woods to see him, because he will often wander into your parks or gardens in the winter, and the thing which will surprise you is the little notice he takes of you. It isn't that he is bold. He doesn't seem to bother whether his hunting brings him close to you or not. He just carries on as if you weren't there, and often you can get so near that you can almost touch him. But he's a sturdy midget, and has even been seen in mid-winter taking a cold plunge in the water running out from a frozen lake! The most wonderful thing about him is his nest. It is minute, a deep cup-shaped ball of the most delicate mosses and lichens, woven together with cobweb and slung like a hammock beneath a branch of a Scots pine or fir-tree. I have found two in one tree. It is thickly lined with soft feathers. As you may imagine, the eggs are tiny, but the hen gold-crest lays as many as ten of them, so there must often be as much overcrowding as there is in the long-tailed tit-mouse home.

Although the gold-crest is a truly British bird, many come as visitors, and how they manage to get here across the North Sea from Norway or Denmark is a bit of a puzzle. It used to be thought that they rode here on the back of some bigger and stronger bird, but that doesn't seem to make sense. What really happens, I think, is that the gold-crest just sets off over the sea, and if he is lucky to have a steady wind under his tail it blows him along nicely to land on our shores. If not, then the poor little chap battles on till he can go no farther, and then plunges into a watery grave. All of which means that of those gold-crests which set out to visit us, only the lucky ones get here.

Now for a long jump. If the gold-crest makes the most beautiful and delicate of nests, the wood-pigeon makes just about the shabbiest and most uncomfortable. It is nothing more than a rickety platform of sticks stuck up in a high hedge or in a tree, so flat that the eggs are in danger of rolling off! Indeed, if you stand below it you can often see the sky, and even the eggs,

KESTREL

GOLD-CREST

through the sticks, so carelessly is it made. The eggs, by the way, are a glossy white, like ping-pong balls, only more pointed. The wood-pigeon lays only two at a time, but as I have already told you, she goes on laying for half the year, one lot after another. Sometimes you may find a nest with young pigeons in it—"squabs," they are called—and they are just about as ugly as the nest— gawky things, covered with greyish whiskers and with black faces. But though you may never have found its nest, it will be odd if you don't already know the wood-pigeon, because, in spite of its name, it is quite as much at home in city streets as country cornfields, and nests just as readily in town buildings as woodland trees. It is as familiar a person in our cities as our policemen, and it has somewhat the same plump, unhurried appearance. It will walk about the streets and parks, right among the traffic, and yet get out of the way of bus and taxi without ever seeming to hurry. It always looks well fed, and so it is. If the truth must be told, the wood-pigeon is both a greedy and an artful person. If you wish to know what sort of an appetite it has got, I can tell you that as many as 1,296 seeds of corn have been found in one bird's crop (which is the name for a bird's stomach). Another crop contained 1,435 grains of buckwheat, and a third 38 hazel nuts! Not only is each wood-pigeon a glutton, which is especially fond of crops like corn and brussel sprouts and other vegetables which are grown to feed us, but it descends on them in large flocks. In winter the myriads of British pigeons are joined by thousands of visitors from overseas, so that the fields sometimes look blue with them. And they are so cunning and watchful that it is not easy for the farmers to keep down their numbers by shooting them. The wood-pigeon is not one of my favourites, but I do love to hear his drowsy cooing on a warm summer's day. It seems to blend with the lazy rustle of the leaves of the trees and the murmuring of the bees.

O.B.B.

H

TURTLE-DOVE

The wood-pigeon has also a sort of snoring call, which I was always told sounded like "Don't scold so, Sally! Don't scold so, Sally! Don't!", though you can make it into what you think fits it best. We once had a French bulldog —you know, one of those small bulldogs with sticking-up ears. Her name was Julie, and we used to imagine the pigeons were saying to her, "Don't snore so, Julie! Don't snore so, Julie!"—which was certainly what should have been said, because she did snore dreadfully. The wood-pigeon is also known as the ring-dove, because of its white collar. Of the other British doves, the stock-dove is not unlike the ring-dove, without a white collar. It is more a bird of open spaces. The turtle-dove is still smaller and is a woodland bird, but it only comes to us in summer from North Africa. The turtle-dove is a gentle fawny-brown person with a black collar, and used to be a great favourite as a pet. The trouble is, that in spite of its delicate appearance, it is almost as greedy and destructive as its blue wood-pigeon cousin.

Now we come to a number of birds which, though they are not true relations, have much the same way of living. These are the tree-creeper, the nuthatch, and the woodpeckers. Though they are all woodland birds, they will give you plenty of chances to see them, because most of them will come into our parks and gardens to hunt for their food from time to time. All have claws specially made, so that they can run up and down trees as easily

as you and I can walk along the ground. All of them can hang on to a bough upside down. It is in their food that they are different. The tree-creeper is a dear little bird, which is far more common than you might think, and the reason you don't see him oftener is because he is such a small and mouse-like person. If you keep your eyes open, you are almost sure, sooner or later, to notice something like a brown mouse running jerkily up or around a tree-trunk, or out along or even under a branch. Having once spotted him, watch him, and you will see what a methodical hunter he is. He is after the tiny grubs and insects which he finds in the bark or cracks of the trees. He takes tree by tree, beginning at the bottom of the trunk and working upwards and then round and round. As soon as he has inspected one tree to his satisfaction he will begin at the bottom of the next. I've never seen a tree-creeper who wasn't busy, everlastingly on the move, poking his longish, slightly curved beak into every nook and crack. The tree-creeper makes its nest in a hole in a tree or behind a loose piece of bark, and lays from five to eight eggs, which are white ones, with reddish-brown spots at the thick end. Young tree-creepers are comical little things, and I was once lucky enough to come on mother tree-creeper giving her babies what looked like a lesson in creeping, but unfortunately I disturbed them, so that I never saw exactly what she *was* teaching them.

The nuthatch is a bigger and much more handsome bird, with its slate-blue coat, chestnut waistcoat, and black eye-streak. Although it is a tree-climber, it is not nearly so methodical as the tree-creeper, dashing all over the trees rather than creeping up them, and coming down head first as easily as it goes up. The explanation is, that while the tree-creeper eats only insects, the nuthatch eats either insects or nuts and seeds. You can tell this from their beaks. The tree-creeper, you will see, has a thin, curved one, which he pokes into holes and crevices to pick out grubs and flies. The nuthatch goes more roughly at the job, and with his stronger, shorter beak, he hammers on the bark till he has prised out an insect, or on a nut till he has got to the kernel. What he usually does with a nut is to take it and wedge it into a crack in a tree. Then, when it is fixed firmly in place, he proceeds to chisel away at it. If you watch him doing this, you can learn how to put your back into a punch at boxing or a lawn-tennis service. He strikes with the full weight of his body behind each blow. First he takes firm hold with his claws, braces himself by pressing his strong tail against the tree, and then—biff—hits with his body, head and beak all in one piece. The tree-creeper chooses what he thinks is a nice-sized hole or crack for his nest. The nuthatch finds a hole he likes, and, if it is too small, carves away at it with his beak till it is big enough for his purpose. If it is too big he shows that he can be a builder, as well as a carpenter, and plasters up the hole with mud till he has made it just the size he wants. So neatly does he do his plastering that you can seldom tell which is plaster and which is tree. In winter he will often come close to houses. A pair of

SPARROW-HAWK

STOCK-DOVE

nuthatches come regularly on to my window sills, and often take a look at us as we are having breakfast. They don't come because they can smell our porridge or bacon, but because the house is an old one, and they have a good idea that they can find some insects or grubs sheltering in the chinks in the walls.

The difference with the woodpeckers is, that they really peck wood for their daily bread and to make their homes. They are the best bird carpenters and carvers. There are three of them in Britain—the green, the greater-spotted, and the lesser-spotted woodpecker—but you are only likely to see the first two, and not them if you live in Scotland or Ireland, where woodpeckers are very rare. Both the green woodpecker and the greater-spotted one will eat things like nuts and acorns, but they prefer insects and grubs. What they do is to examine a tree, climbing up and around it in much the same way as the tree-creeper and the nuthatch, but tapping on it all the time with their very strong, sharp beaks. They are not satisfied only with the insects they find on the bark, they want to get at those which have bored into the tree. Wood which has become riddled with insects or their grubs or caterpillars soon becomes rotten, if it wasn't rotten before, and the woodpeckers know this. So they go tap-tapping till they come to a place which gives out the hollow sound of rotten wood. Then they set to work. You have all seen men working on the roads with one of those drills, which go brrrrr! brrrrr! and fairly eat into the

NUTHATCH

TREE-CREEPER

hardest concrete or pavement. The woodpecker uses his beak to do the same thing to a tree, and it goes as fast as the drill, so fast that if you watched him you could not tell how quickly he was hitting. When he has bored down to the grub he knew was there, he shoots out his long sticky tongue, catches the grub in it, and, thank you very much, there's a tasty morsel for Mr. Woodpecker himself, or to take back to the young woodpeckers which Mrs. Woodpecker has hatched off in a neat hole which the pair of them have specially drilled into a tree. To begin with you are probably more likely to find woodpeckers' holes, all round and neatly drilled, than to see the woodpeckers themselves. But the green woodpecker particularly should not be difficult to spot, because he has a habit of coming on to fields, or even lawns, in search of ants or other insects. If he does, don't disturb him, but watch how he fairly thumps his beak into the earth. He is a handsome fellow, with a greeny-yellow suit and scarlet crest, and he has a cheerful, laughing sort of a call, from which he gets his name of "Yaffle." You can recognise him also by his flight, as he flies in a series of swoops, up for a little, then down, then up again. He is rather partial to ants, and if you live where there are many ants' nests you may one day come on him tearing them in pieces and eating the ants and their eggs. The greater-spotted woodpecker is also a handsome bird, but he is shyer than the green one, and sticks more to the woods, where his colouring makes it more difficult to pick him out easily. He has a habit of calling up his wife or friends by drumming with his beak on a hollow tree. He makes a noise just like the roll of drums, which shows how quickly his beak must move and what a strong neck he must have. I doubt whether many of you will be able to get at a woodpecker's nest, because it is usually quite a way below the hole. Even if you get up to the hole, you won't be able to reach down to the nest without making the hole bigger, and that means sawing or chiselling it, and so ruining the woodpecker's home. To save you the trouble of upsetting a woodpecker family, I can tell you the nest is a most uninteresting affair of woodchips and sawdust. and the eggs are dead white.

So far all the birds we have talked about have been good characters. Some may be cheeky, some quick tempered, and not a few both greedy and destructive in our gardens and on our farms. But they are people who, by and large, are content to live and let other birds live. Now we have got to think about those which attack other birds' eggs and young, and which eat the flesh of birds and animals. Nature made them that way, so that it is not their fault, and, indeed, if there were not these robber and killer birds, it is likely that we should have plagues of smaller birds and beasts which would do enormous damage. I wouldn't like to see hundreds of great tit-mice making a mass raid on my poor bees, nor would the farmers who grow the corn for our bread be pleased if the ripening ears were eaten off by thousands of sparrows. Birds like crows and hawks and owls do good as well as harm. Not only do they keep down the numbers of the smaller birds, but they kill and eat all kinds of destructive animals like rats, mice and beetles. Of course they can easily do a lot of harm if their numbers are not checked, but we see to it that they are. Sometimes this is a pity, and there are birds which in the bad old days were hunted down so hard that they have almost disappeared. But nowadays we are more careful, and try to do no more than keep the numbers of robbers and killers within limits.

The crows are all robbers. They will rob for the sake of robbing, and will eat almost anything that their tummies can digest—and some things which it doesn't seem they could!—whether it be a dead animal, the eggs or babies of smaller birds, or acorns, corn, or even vegetables. Don't expect songs from the crow tribe. They are croakers and screechers, which make no attempt at singing. None of them are gentle birds, and the fiercer and wilder members of the tribe, like the raven and the hooded carrion crows, have been driven so far away into the wild places that you are not often likely to come across them. They are huge blackish birds, though their plumage is really far from black. They live to be very old, and they have a rough sort of grunting bark. When I tell you that the raven will kill and eat young lambs or even sick sheep as well as rabbits and small birds of all kinds, you will not wonder why it has been chased away from our houses and farmlands. The crows which you can see and watch if you are lucky—for all crows are shy and suspicious, as well they should be—are the rook, the jackdaw, the magpie, and the jay. All these

TAWNY-OWL

ROOK'S HEAD—POUCH FULL OF FOOD

we have already mentioned, but we had better take a close-up view of them. You can always recognise the rook, as I have told you, by his bald face. This bald look is given because he has no feathers on his cheeks and throat, which form a sort of elastic pouch, which Father and Mother Rook stuff with food until it is bulging. Then they fly off to their nests and shovel it straight into their babies' beaks. They go on feeding them like this long after the young ones have left the nest, and what gobbles of joy there are while the feeding is going on! To give the rook his due, he is more of a vegetarian than his cousins, and seldom bothers to rob small birds. His crime is that he does a lot of damage in cornfields, but, if we are fair to him, we must admit that most of the plants

RAVEN

JACKDAW

he digs up have already been attacked at their roots by some horrid insect like a wireworm or a leather-jacket, and it is this tasty mouthful, and not the corn itself, which the rook is after.

In many ways the jackdaw is like a smaller rook, except that he is more perky and not so shabby looking, and has a nice round grey head, instead of that ugly long beak and those bald cheeks. Like the rook, he is all for company, and you will seldom find a jackdaw nesting alone. Several families nest close together, usually in old trees or ruined buildings or in cliffs by the sea, but they are not so open about their home-building, and generally make some attempt to hide their nests. Sometimes the jackdaw will make his nest in a chimney, and then he is a perfect nuisance. He brings twigs and sticks, which he drops down the chimney-pot, thinking he will fill up the hole. Of course, its usually too long and too big, but he doesn't know that, so goes on carrying and dropping sticks till he has made a beastly mess, and probably blocked up the chimney lower down. He is a great sticker, and sometimes succeeds more by good luck than hard work in blocking a chimney near enough to the top so that he can make his nest there. He will pinch young birds or eggs whenever he can, but he also likes corn and an occasional meal of fruit. He doesn't object to a juicy insect either, and you may often see him sitting on the backs of sheep, hunting for the ticks in the sheep's wool. That at least is a friendly action, because these ticks worry the sheep dreadfully. The jackdaw loves thieving. He will try and steal a bone from a dog, or even some little thing you or I may have left about. Still, he is not the champion sneak-thief

that his first cousin the magpie is. Magpies will steal for the joy of stealing, and are especially attracted by anything shiny or silvery—spoons, forks, silver coins, any old trinket which glints in the sunshine, they will snap up and carry off to their nests. I knew one which was watched making regular visits to a lady's dressing-table through her bedroom window, until it had flown away with everything on it that it could carry. That, by the way, was a tame magpie. Both magpies and jackdaws make amusing pets, because you need not keep them caged all the time. Like the ravens at the Tower of London, they will get tame enough to roam about round your house or in the yard, but don't keep one if you are in the habit of leaving your treasures lying about!

The magpie is a comical bird, and in its dress of black and white reminds me of Pierrot. I should not really call it black and white, for what looks black at a distance gleams with brilliant green and violet lights when seen close-to. We have got to admit that, in spite of his bad habits, the magpie is a handsome person, and a graceful one too, with a dipping flight and a perky way of flirting his long tail like a fan. He makes his nest in trees or tall hedges. It is the usual crow bundle of sticks and twigs, but with the difference that it has a sort of roof over it to keep out the rain. It used to be thought unlucky to see a single magpie, and my mother, who came from Ireland, used to tell me "One for sorrow, two for joy," and that I should take off my hat when I saw one. In those days magpies were scarce, and you seldom saw more than two at a time, though over in France, where the magpie came from into England, you can often see parties of fifteen or more. If I had followed her advice when I was in France I should have been raising my hat almost all the time! Although they are shot and trapped because of the damage they do, the magpies are increasing in numbers in Britain. So, too, are the jays. This is the more surprising, since the jay, being the most dreadful egg-thief, is especially fond of pheasant's eggs. If you remember what I told you about the way pheasants are protected and their enemies killed, you may be sure that fierce war is waged on jays. Yet they are so shy and so cunning that they are most difficult to shoot and even to trap. They live almost entirely in woods, and rarely venture far outside the cover of trees. Long before you have seen one you will probably have heard a harsh scream of "Craak! Craak!" coming out of the depths of a big wood. That will be Mr. Jay having a gentle conversation with his wife, telling her, most likely, that he has found a hedge-sparrow's nest with young ones, or a clutch of khaki pheasant's eggs. A trap baited with a pheasant's egg is about the best way of catching the jay; but he is almost as bad a friend to the gardener as he is to game birds. He will come into gardens very early in the morning, long before we have thought of getting up, and pick off a whole row of peas or broad-beans. One old man I knew used to grow prize broad-beans to enter at vegetable shows. Whacking great things they were, and he used to spend hours watering, training, and manuring them. Then one night a jay arrived, spied those lucious monsters with his cold blue eye, and cleared off the lot! The best

BARN-OWL.

HOVERING KESTREL

we can say about the jay is that he is handsome but horrid, and not only is he handsome but unusual. He is, as you see, the only British crow which has a rich pinky uniform instead of the usual blue-black, grey or white.

If the crows are robbers the hawks and owls are killers, living almost entirely on other birds, beasts, and insects. All of them, as you will see, have beaks and claws specially hooked and sharp for catching, killing, and tearing. They are savage people, and their eyes have the same fierce yellow look that you will see in the tiger or the leopard. The hawks are a large family. At one end there are the eagles, but to-day our only British eagle—the golden eagle—has, as I have said, been banished to the highest mountains of Scotland. The other hawks can be divided into two kinds—those with pointed wings, which are properly called falcons, and those which have rounder wings. As you are very seldom likely to see a hawk except in flight, this will help you to know which is which. The only two hawks which can be ranked among our acquaintances are the kestrel and the sparrow-hawk. Both are common birds, in spite of the way in which they are hunted.

The kestrel, which is perhaps the commoner of the two, is a falcon. As you will see, he is a beautiful creature, with wonderful powers of hovering poised in the sky, from which he gets his nickname of "Windhover." Once you've seen him perform this marvellous feat you will never mistake him. It is difficult to explain exactly what he does. He will fly easily along, even in a high wind, when suddenly from his height above the ground his quick eyes spot something moving—a mouse, a beetle, or a pheasant chick maybe—in the grass or stubbles far below him. To make quite sure, he suddenly stops flying and sort of back-pedals, fanning the air with his wings. For a moment or two he stays quite still, hanging in the sky and watching. Perhaps he is mistaken. He then flies or glides on for a bit. Again he thinks he sees something, and again he puts on the brake and hangs over the place. Then, head foremost, he dives straight down, seizes his prey, and up again, and away to eat it somewhere. It is a wonderful performance, which no other bird can do anything like as well. The trick is how he is able to hover like that and then plunge so quickly. In olden days our ancestors used to make falcons hunt for them. What they did was to catch and train young falcons— the great goshawk and peregrine falcons as well as the smaller kestrels and still smaller merlins— as hunters. When they were trained, the falconer would go out into the country with the falcon sitting on his wrist, blindfolded by wearing a little hood over its eyes. When he saw in the distance some bird which was good to eat, like a partridge or a duck, he would take off the hood and throw the falcon into the air. As soon as the falcon spotted the bird it would attack and kill it, and all the falconer had to do was to collect the bird and put back the hood on his falcon until he saw another suitable victim. Of course, when the falcon had done its day's work, it was taken back to its cage and given a good feed. Falconry, as this hunting with hawks is called, is still done by a few people, and one Englishman has even trained a great golden eagle to hunt for him. There is no doubt that the kestrel does some good by eating mice and beetles, but he is not liked, because he is as likely to kill the chicks of game birds and sometimes small birds. It is not strictly a woodland bird, for you may see it almost anywhere in fields, on the moors, or by the sea as well as in wooded districts. It makes its nest high up in places where you will very seldom be able to reach it (the same as all the hawks and crows), in tall trees, church towers, old ruins or rocky crags. The eggs are worth mentioning, because they are a lovely reddish-chocolate colour, not unlike those of the red grouse.

The sparrow-hawk has rounded wings, but if you ever see him perching you will think of him as a taller, longer-legged bird than the kestrel. When he is flying, you can easily tell him not only by his wings, but by the way he

PEREGRINE FALCON

BUZZARD

dashes along a hedge or through the thickest woods, fairly close to the ground. He doesn't soar or hover, but just flies smack into a lot of sparrows or on to a brood of baby chickens, strikes one down with his beak, and then stands on it and eats it. This blind dash may lead him into trouble, and he has been known to crash badly against a tree or a window-pane, and sometimes to kill himself. The sparrow-hawk will eat mice, beetles, and frogs, but will attack birds even as big as a wood-pigeon as well as the smaller ones. You can imagine that it is not popular with farmers or game-breeders, but it, too, does good as well as harm. It is far more a woodland bird than a kestrel, and nests in tall trees, often taking over the last year's nest of some crow or other bird.

Another distant relation of the hawks which we ought to mention is the buzzard, for although he used to be very rare, he is now under kinder treatment becoming more common, and you may see him in Devon and Cornwall, in Wales, and in parts of Scotland and Ireland. He is a biggish, round-looking bird, whose call is something like the "miee-you" of a kitten. He does far more good than harm, and if he does occasionally snap up a careless bird, he is generally content to feed on mice, moles, and young rabbits.

The buzzard always seems to me to be half-way between a hawk and an owl, for the owls are really no more than hawks which hunt by night. They are, of course, very distant relations, and don't look at all like hawks, except that they have the same cruel hooked beaks and the same strong, sharp claws for seizing and tearing. You all know what they look like from pictures—comical, round people, with great big rings of feathers round their eyes and a very serious wise look, but don't imagine you can get to know owls from books. When I was a boy I was lucky, because some people near-by had a tame owl in a cage. I spent hours watching it and feeding it with dead mice, and have loved owls ever since. Owls are creatures of the night—though some do go about in the daytime—and so are usually more often heard than seen. Because of this and because most of them have weird cries, some boys and girls may not like owls. They may even be frightened at the hoots and screams which come suddenly out of the darkness before they have gone to sleep, but you must never worry about these. They are nothing more than the calls of our two commonest owls. The hoot of "Hoo-hoo-hoo!" with a kind of quaver in the last note, is made by the tawny owl. The barn-owl makes a startling noise, which begins with a hiss, and then rises to a sort of cross between a snore and a scream! People say that owls utter these horrid cries to help them in their hunting. They are soft and silent flyers—when you see one flying you will think its wings are padded with cotton wool—and the idea is that they glide up to a bush or down towards the grass and then let out a loud hoot or scream. This scares the bird or mouse that is hiding there, and it dashes out in panic, only to be seized by the owl. Well, that may or may not be true, but it is a good story anyway, and the owls must have some reason for their nightly noises, which you will be sure to hear whether you live in town or country. How, you may ask, does an owl see to hunt on even the darkest night? The answer is found in those great round eye-pieces. In the daytime most owls have a sleepy look, but that's only because their eyes are half-closed in daylight, just as you and I have to screw ours up in strong sunlight. If you are quick to notice things, you will see that birds have their eyes set one on either side of their heads, so that they have to cock their heads sideways to look at you. The owl's eyes are different—they both face forward. When wide open they look big, but you can only see part of them, the greater part being hidden inside the bird's skull. It will surprise you to learn that an owl's eye is bigger than a grown-up man's! Not only is this eye big and strong, but the ring of feathers surrounding it acts as a reflector, helping it to make use of every scrap of light, so that the owl can fly about as easily in darkness as we can run about in daylight. There are two other funny things about an owl's eyes. First, his eyelids shut down from above to close its eyes like ours do, and not up from underneath like other birds. Next, his eyes are so firmly fixed in its head that when it wishes to look to one side or another it doesn't move its eyes but turns its whole head. Try this out by walking round an owl when you find one perching up in a tree, and you will see that he follows you with his head, which

LONG-EARED OWL   SHORT-EARED OWL

he can screw round so far that he is almost looking backwards. There is such a lot to know about owls. They will eat beetles, rats, mice, small birds, or the young of the bigger birds. Their way of digesting them is very odd. They just gobble up the whole mouse, bird, or beetle—fur, feathers, bones, claws, and all. But the owl keeps in his tummy only the meat, and sicks up the bones and fur and whatnots rolled up in nice little balls or pellets. You may often be led to find where an owl is living by these pellets scattered under a tree or old wall. You are surely likely to come across the tawny-owl and the barn-owl. The tawny-owl is a real woodland bird. Another name for it is the wood-owl, and it makes its nest in a hole in a tree, a ruined building, an old pigeon's nest, or even in a rabbit-hole. The eggs, like those of all owls, are white and round. The barn-owl may live in woods, but, I think, prefers to come closer to our dwellings, and favourite nesting-places are barns, farmyard buildings, ivy-covered ruins, or church towers. He is sometimes known as the white owl, because he looks white when he is flying. Very ghostly and white he looks sometimes at night as he flops silently out of a dark stump or thick ivy and flies off into the darkness.

Another owl which you are almost sure to see is the little owl. He is a foreigner, who has only been in Britain about sixty years and has managed to get himself a bad reputation. Perhaps that's because we don't take kindly to foreigners: perhaps he has been unfairly blamed for taking young game chicks. But he has his champions, and there are people who have set out to prove he does nothing but good, living only on beetles and such-like insects. Well, look at him. Can you imagine such a flat-headed, fierce-eyed, frowning little person being a saint? He is a daylight hunter, though he also kills at night, and he has a big appetite. You will often see something which looks like a round blob on a branch or a post-and-rail fence. As you get closer it drops off and flies away. This will be a little owl. You can also recognise its sort of mewing call.

There are lots of other owls, but few of them are common. The most comical are the long-eared owl, with his two tufts, which look like ears but aren't; and the short-eared owl, which always reminds me of the owl which went to sea with the Pussycat "in a beautiful pea-green boat." This owl is sometimes called the "woodcock owl," which brings me to the last of our possible acquaintances in trees and woods—the woodcock.

The woodcock always seems to me a mystery bird, and though you may often pass close to one in a deep wood you are not often likely to see it. In figure and form he is like his cousin the snipe (whom we shall meet later when we talk about water-birds), and he feeds in wet marshy places, but for some reason he insists on living and nesting in thick woods where there is plenty of bracken and brambles and such plants for him to hide in. All day long he will skulk about among them, his barred plumage exactly matching the brown bracken and dark shadows. If you frighten him out he will only flutter into the open for a second or two, then flap off on a silent, owl-like flight between the trees and flop back again into cover. Yet at night he creeps out to some nice wet place by river or lake, and uses his long, delicate beak to catch his supper of worms. He does this by pushing his beak into the soft earth and turning it from side to side, feeling for worms. Its nest is usually on the ground, though the only one I have found was on the trunk of a fallen tree. If the hen woodcock knows her nest has been found when she has her babies in it, she will move them off somewhere else, though no one is quite sure how she does this. She must carry them in her beak, but how she holds them is not certainly known. The woodcock, like the plover, is also an actor, and will sham hurt to lead you away from its nest.

LITTLE OWL

Chapter V

OF RIVER, MARSH AND SHORE

WE have seen that, when we have made friends which inhabit our gardens or parks, we have to start taking walks into country lanes, fields, and woods to meet those which live there. Many of these will often oblige us by coming into our gardens or the parks of city or town. Kestrels and owls, for example, as well as pigeons, sparrows, and others, nest regularly in the middle of London. But unless you are lucky enough to live close by a river or lake or at the seaside, you will have to make special expeditions to see the birds of river, marsh, and shore, especially if you wish to find their nests, which are usually difficult to reach unless you can swim or don't mind getting very wet and bedraggled. For this reason these birds may not perhaps so easily become familiar to you as those you see more easily and can watch more often, but they are most interesting and beautiful people.

I think the best way we can get a good view of them will be to follow a river down from the place where it begins until it empties itself into the sea. You probably all know that a river starts as a spring, which bubbles out of some far-away hillside, a thin trickle of clear water which tinkles down from stone to stone. It is joined by the trickles from other springs and becomes a brooklet, chattering to itself as it runs over its pebbly bed. It soon widens into what you may call a brook, a beck, or a burn, depending on where you live, and as it goes is met by other brooks, each of which swells its waters, until by the time it has left the hills and has reached flatter country it has become a river. The soil through which it runs is now softer and less rocky and so is easier washed away. The banks are no longer steep, and the result is that the river grows broader and flows more slowly. In places it overflows and forms either marshy land or lakes and ponds. These are fringed with tall reeds and rushes, plants and bushes, which form wonderful hide-outs for water-loving birds of all sorts. The river may, of course, then pass through some big town and become all dirty and horrible, but at last it nears the sea, and its

WOODCOCK

YELLOW WAGTAIL

flat banks become flatter and covered with rough grasses and perhaps a few scrubby bushes. As its fresh waters running down meet the salt water of the sea, the mouth of the river, as it is called, becomes very wide at high tide. But when the tide goes out again the river waters are left winding their way to the sea between stretches of mud—mud-flats—which are covered with water at high tide. These are the hunting-grounds of birds without number. The mud is full of sea-snails, slugs, and worms, all of which make the most scrumptious meals for an army of birds, some of which we have met already —like the lapwing and the curlew.

The reason I have told you all this is to explain why I have divided the water-loving birds first into birds of the river—that is, the top part of the river from the spring where it starts until it enters the flat country. Secondly, the birds of the marsh—that is, all those which live in the reeds, rushes, and bushes of the swampy ground round the slow-flowing river. Thirdly, the birds you will see among the rough grasses or on the mud-banks where the river joins the sea, or on the seashore.

Let's take a walk along the brook as it tumbles down the hillside. You will see it is very shallow where it swirls and froths between rocks, but deep and still in the dark pools where the banks overhang. The first birds you see you will recognise as acquaintances you have already made—grey and yellow wag-tails, both looking very yellow and canaryish in the sunlight; and if you look upwards you may spy a kestrel hovering as if he were anchored in the sky. But who is that plump small bird hopping easily on the rocks sticking out of the racing water, balancing and bobbing little curtsies? From stone to stone he goes bobbing and dipping, a habit which gives him his name of dipper. In his black suit and white shirt-front he reminds you of a waiter in a restaurant —but he is far more nimble. Watch him as he comes to where the water falls over a rocky ledge into the pool below. He just dodges through the water, or behind it, then straight into the pool he walks. If you are ever able to get close enough, you may (though it's not likely) see him doing his famous trick of swimming under water. He uses his wings for swimming as well as for flying, and seems almost to walk through the bottom of the pool. Of course

KINGFISHERS

he cannot really do that, but he can, and does, move about easily in and under water. The odd thing is that he doesn't dive but just walks in—and out! In a crack in the overhanging bank of the pool you may find his nest, often placed quite close to the water. Quite a comfortable house it is too. It looks at first to be a domed one, like the wren's, but the dome is really a sort of outer shell, made of moss or grass and lichens to prevent the nest getting wet. The entrance hole is low down at the side, and the nest itself, where the white eggs are laid, is built of grasses, and isn't unlike a blackbird's.

The dipper is also called a water-ousel, but this isn't a good name, because it will muddle you up with the ring-ousel, which is quite a different bird and no relation at all. He is a visiting member of the thrush family, rather like a blackbird, with a white-ringed collar on its throat. He is a bird which is only found in moorland country, but he is fond of water, and never likes to be far from a brook or burn.

Almost anywhere along the course of a river you may find the kingfisher —the "compleat angler," as much at home in the shallows of a brook, the idly flowing stream of a big river, or the still waters of lake or pond. In my garden there is a sort of small lake, a stretch of rather muddy water surrounded by trees, but kingfishers come to it regularly, especially when near-by ponds are dried up. I can watch the birds from my bathroom window. The odd thing is how different they may appear. When the sun catches them they flash like blue jewels across the gloomy water, their wings whirring so fast you cannot see them. At other times they look almost black. The kingfisher is the most brilliant of all British birds, almost foreign looking in his blaze of blue-green and chestnut-pink. One of the loveliest bird-sights I ever saw was a pair of

kingfishers whirring and wheeling high up in the sky above a clump of dark Scots firs. Often you could not see them as birds. They were just flying streaks of glistening blue and silver. Twenty-five yards from my house stands an aged oak tree, one great branch of which stretches over the water. This is a favourite perch for the kingfisher, so it is most convenient for me to watch him. For a long time he will sit quite still, except that he turns his head first to one side and then to the other, then looks into the water about eight feet below him. Suddenly down he falls, quite straight—straighter than you or I or any aeroplane could dive. In a flash he is up again on his bough. The whole dive down and up seems to take no more than a second, but each time he has his breakfast in his sharp beak, usually a minnow or a young roach. He will eat insects and tadpoles and water-snails, but I fancy he prefers fish whenever he can get them. The kingfisher makes its home in a tunnel into the bank of river or lake, but when you find it you will get a bit of a shock to find what a badly kept, evil-smelling place it is. This comes of the kingfisher's somewhat careless way of digesting its fishy meals. Rather like the owls, they are inclined to bolt their food and then throw up the bony, skinny parts which they cannot digest. You can imagine how this fishy mess can smell after a week or so, especially shut up in a three-foot tunnel where there is not much air! The kingfisher doesn't really make a proper nest, but lays four white eggs at the end of the tunnel among all the mess and fish-bones. It's odd that children brought up in such dirt and smell can turn out so beautiful.

If you can find the kingfisher anywhere along the course of a river, the same applies to the heron. You are never sure where you will not see a heron—in the reeds by the river, a pool left by the tide on the seashore, or even in the most grubby little ditch. I have told you how I saw one in the middle of London. The truth is, that he will go anywhere there is water, for he knows that in water, or near water, he will always be sure to find food. In the brook, he may take a young trout or a frog; from the river, a roach or a water-rat or a young moorhen; in the ditch, a fat water-beetle; and on the seashore, any fish or sea-snail that he comes across. He is a sort of stork, with his long legs and neck and spear of a beak. I imagine that, until you know how to spot him, he will see you long before you see him, and the first impression you will have of him is of a harsh croak of alarm and then of a big French-grey bird rising steeply but with slow flapping wings from the reeds, his lanky legs trailing beneath him. Watch him as he beats his way across the sky, his head tucked back, his legs a-trail. If he hasn't been really scared, he will soon glide down again, alight very gently for so big a bird, and walk carefully forward for two or three steps. Having found a nice place, probably with his legs in the water, he "freezes"—that is, he keeps dead still and waits—just waits until some fish or frog comes swimming near enough for him to pounce like a flash and pierce it on that sharp beak. Unless you have seen him alight and take up his position you will find it difficult to watch him. He will just "brood like a ghost and as still as a post" for hours, and his greyness blends exactly with his surroundings. The trouble about him—and the kingfisher, of course—is that he does kill a lot of fish, big ones as well as small, but I think we should be generous and allow him these, although, of course, his appetite does mean that there may be fewer fish for the fishermen to catch. Like the rook, the heron nests in colonies, called heronries. In high trees they make huge nests of sticks, and lay about four or five pale greeny-blue eggs in them.

It is when the brook has broadened into a river flowing through flat marshy places or lakes or ponds that the number of water-birds really begins to grow large. These wet places give cover to all kinds of birds—little perchers, larger waders and ducks, snipe and redshank, heron and hawk. The snipe nesting in the soggy meadows knows that it will be a damp and dirty job for you to hunt for his nest. The perching birds, like the reed-bunting—a first cousin to our old acquaintance of the fields, the yellow-hammer—are fairly sure you will be scratched by brambles and stung by mosquitoes, as well as nettles, if you try and reach the sedge where they are nesting. The waders—moorhens, coots, and grebes—all know that it will be very unlikely you can reach their nests without a boat or a bathing suit. Lastly, the ducks smile to themselves in their comical way because, though you may see them on the water or in the reeds, they are careful to make their nests in dry places, often in a wood and sometimes up a tree. A swamp on the lake's edge is a tangled mass of thorn,

HERON

DABCHICK

sallow, or alder trees; of brambles, nettles, and rough grass; and of tall, plumed reeds and rushes, standing with their feet in the water. It is usually a place into which inquisitive people cannot easily poke their noses or their feet or fingers to interfere with the birds who live there. Also, it gives those birds plenty of chance to hide their nests, and, most important, plenty of lovely juicy food.

Four birds you will be almost sure to see are the moorhen, his first cousin, the coot, and his not-too-distant relations, the grebes. The moorhen, or water-hen, is found almost anywhere there is water, except, perhaps, in the fast-flowing brooks or rivulets. His name is muddling. It comes from mere-hen —that is, a bird of the mere (which is another name for a small lake), and not the moors. You can spot moorhens on practically every river. You will probably hear them first. They have a sharp little cry that sounds something like "Chrrrick!" and a kind of squawk. The thing you will see first is most likely to be two little patches of white vanishing into the reeds. Those are the moor-hen's tail feathers. He has seen you and he is off—for the moment. But he is an impudent person, and will soon step carefully out of hiding again. He doesn't like to be caught in the open, because he is a very poor flier. He has to taxi along like a seaplane before he can take off properly, and as he goes his feet trail in the water. They are quick-tempered people, so that, though you may find lots of them along a biggish river or a large lake, the rule is: one small pond, one pair of moorhens. In my part of England, almost every field has its little pond, and each one is owned by a pair of moorhens. If any others come they are at once attacked and driven away. They are a perfect pest to the gardener. In the dusk of spring or summer evenings I can see one or two stealing from the lake towards the kitchen garden. Sometimes, if I get up very early, I catch them creeping back again to the water. You don't need to ask what they have been doing! Eating off my lettuce and cabbage plants

—that's all! So I make war on them to stop them becoming too many. I try and shoot some of those which wander in from the fields, and if I can find the nest of the pair which live on my lake, we take their eggs and eat them. Jolly good they are too. Both the moorhen and the coot make much the same kind of nest—a biggish, strong affair of reeds, flags, and grasses. The coot nearly always builds his up in the water or among the reeds, but the moorhen's is normally found closer to the bank and sometimes up a tree. The moorhen, I may say, is a champion climber, and can run up a wire fence as cleverly as a monkey. The eggs of both birds are much the same, both being of a sort of stone colour with spots. The moorhen's eggs are slightly smaller and more sandy. The spots are red or brown while those on the coot's eggs are black or blackish. Both birds lay a lot of eggs—up to a dozen or more.

The moorhen will push his way into gardens, but you will have to go in search of the coot. He is quite common, but he keeps to the wide stretches of water or to slow-flowing, reed-fringed rivers. If the first thing you notice about a moorhen is his white tail, the first thing that will strike you about the coot is his white forehead. This gives him a bald look, and you may hear people say that Mr. So-and-so is "as bald as a coot." Although the coot is a fairly shy person, he fights fiercely with others of his kind. When two of them are scrapping they make a great fuss about it, rushing at each other in the water, squawking and splashing.

The grebes are a family of birds which are far more at home in the water than on land. They are like submarines—they can swim a long way under water, and also half under water, so that only their heads and necks are showing. If you come suddenly on one, it may fly off for a few yards, then dive straight into the water. All you can see is a chain of bubbles rising to the surface, and where the bird will bob up will surprise you. The commonest is the little grebe, whose other name is the dabchick. He is a darkish-brown bird, very round and plump, with hardly any tail. You are likely to see him on almost any decent-sized piece of water, but because he is so small, so shy, and so quick, he may not catch your eye like his much less common cousin, the great-crested grebe. Here, if you like, is a comical-looking bird. Look at him! As he bobs up from the water, his longish neck, the fringe of black whiskers round his face, and his ear-like tufts, give him a most absurd look. He seems all wrong, as if someone had stuck a long-eared owl's face on to a duck's neck. I am sure that some people who suddenly see his head and neck pop out of the water must think that they have seen a sort of sea-serpent! Except that his face is so comical, he is a handsome bird, with the most lovely silky breast feathers. In olden times he used to be hunted and killed for this "grebe-fur," and, like the bearded tit-mouse and other birds, had almost disappeared. Nowadays we know better than to be so unkind, and the result is that the number of great crested grebes in Britain is steadily growing, and a very good thing, too, because they are not only handsome but interesting. For

DIPPER
GREY WAGTAIL

GREAT CRESTED GREBE

one thing, both Father and Mother Grebe take turns to sit on the eggs, and, for another, they have a delightful habit of taking their young ones for rides on their backs. It is a very pretty sight to see Mrs. Grebe with two tiny downy babies sitting between her wings. Of course, it is hard luck on them if mother gets scared, because she dives at once, and the two scraps are left bobbing in the water. But she soon comes back to pick them up again. Another interesting thing about the grebes is that they build floating nests, which they anchor to a water-lily root or stalk of reed. It's not a beautiful nest. In fact, it is just a squelchy mass of rotten weeds, rather like a dish of spinach you may have for your dinner. Whenever the grebes leave it they cover the eggs over, so although when you come across one you may think it is just a lump of rubbish or at best an old nest, you are often likely to find it has eggs under the filth. The eggs are queer, too, because though when they are laid they are a nice palish blue, they soon get all stained with slush from the rotting weeds. This at last forms a kind of dirty outer shell over the egg, like the fur you may find inside kettles in districts where the water is hard.

The snipe is first cousin to the woodcock, whom we have met already—very like him to look at, only smaller. The difference is that the snipe lives in swampy meadows near the water instead of in the woods. Like the woodcock it has a very sensitive beak, which it pushes into soft, boggy ground, and feels about for worms and grubs. Years ago my home was only separated from a small river by two water-meadows where the grass grew tall and green. These were full of snipe. It was the most lovely thing to come home from stuffy London in the spring and lie in bed, feel the cool breeze blowing off the water, and listen to the cries of the birds as they came out to have their midnight feasts and to fly about high in the evening sky. I cannot quite describe the cry of the snipe. It is a comforting, queer little call, but the noise which I love he doesn't make with his voice at all. This is a sort of whirring sound, which is called "drumming." What happens is that the happy bird, climbing swiftly

SNIPE

into the air, suddenly turns and dives downwards. As he falls, the wind rushing through his stiff wing and tail feathers makes a kind of whirring rattle. You can make something of the same noise if you blow through tissue paper stretched on a hair-comb, or even through a strong feather. But you will never really imitate that comfortable, glad sound that you will hear day or night when snipe are nesting in the spring of the year. The snipe are great flyers. They go very fast, but they don't go straight. They twist and turn —"jinking," it is called, like a footballer side-steps as he runs. This jerky, jinking flight makes them very difficult targets, so, because they are also good to eat, they are much shot at. You may be pleased to know that there are far more cartridges wasted on snipe than there are birds killed. It takes a good game-shot to hit the little snipe. We used to walk over the water-meadows almost every day hunting for nests. I was never much good at finding them, but my elk-hound was a wizard. All I had to do was to send her off. Her idea was to kill the little shrew-mice which lived in the grass, but as she hunted for them, her quick nose smelt out each nest she came across. She never touched the nest, but whenever I saw her stop and sniff I walked up, and there, under a tussock, would be a shallow scoop, lined with grass, and in it four lovely olive-green and brown eggs, much like the plovers, both in colour and in the way they were arranged, with their sharp ends pointing inwards. When the snipe fly, they often do so in small parties called " wisps."

I should tell you here that many gatherings of birds have special names. I have already mentioned that a lot of starlings is called a "murmuration," and a family party of partridges a "covey." So, when you see several snipe together, you say—if you wish to be correct—a " wisp of snipe." You can talk about a "charm of finches," a "skein of geese," a "host of sparrows," a "spring of teal," a "congregation of plovers," and, funniest of all, a "herd of wrens!"

There are many of these names for a collection of birds—nouns of assembly, they are called—which are no more than pretty inventions, but some, including those I have mentioned, are authentic enough.

In those same water-meadows there used also to be redshank, so called, of course, because their long shanks of legs are red. Though redshank are fairly common, you will not see them just anywhere. They should be found on most rivers, especially where these broaden out into mud-flats before reaching the sea. The bird is about half-way between a snipe and a curlew, and has a weird bubbling call, which always reminds me of the curlew. It is nothing like as good a flier as either of these birds, but it has a queer trick of sort of hopping into the air and down again, rising and alighting in almost the same place. It, too, makes its nest on the ground, but usually in wetter places than the snipe. It lays the usual four eggs, which you will find difficult to tell from those of a plover, except that they are smaller.

> "All along the backwater,
>   Through the rushes tall,
>   Ducks are a'dabbling,
>   Up tails all."

If you have ever read the wonderful adventures of the boastful Mr. Toad in the *Wind in the Willows* you will remember this song about ducks. Ducks are just about the first birds we get to know. Even tiny babies have Donald Duck dolls, and can say "quack-quack" as soon as they can talk. Ducks are lovable people.

> "O Ducks are beautiful things,
>   But Ducks are comical things,
>   As comical as you.
>   Quack!
>   They waddle round, they do,
>   They eat all manner of things,
>   And then they Quack."

They are friendly. They look on us almost as another sort of themselves. Do you remember the old saying that "a dog looks up to you, a cat looks down on you, but a pig looks upon you as another human being?" Well, the duck looks upon you as another larger and perhaps stupider duck. If you won't believe me, watch the way he turns his yellow eye on you, screwing his head round on his neck to get a better view. When he has had a good long look he will just say "Quack!" or it may be "Quaaack!" and walk away. He has summed you up anyway. Oh, by the way, do you know it is only the ducks which quack? The drakes, as the male ducks are called, can only make a thin, dry

MOORHENS

COOT

sound, very feeble and uninteresting, as if they were trying to quack but had sore throats.

I am lucky because I have lots of wild ducks which have become tame. What happened was, that someone gave me a pair of mallards—that is our commonest kind of duck, about which I told you something early on—and I bought some tufted ducks. The mallards laid eggs and hatched off families, and next year these, too, laid eggs, so that in a short time I had lots and lots of tame ducks. We had to cut their wings, of course, otherwise they would have flown away as soon as they were old enough; and also we have to kill them, not only to eat, but to keep down their numbers. Anyway, these mallards especially, are far tamer than any ordinary farmyard Aylesbury or Khaki-Campbell (that's another kind of tame duck, which is khaki in colour and is a good layer of eggs). You cannot believe how tame they are! They will invade the house in a shouting, quacking drove, and have to be chased out. Out of doors they will

REDSHANK

sit down all round our feet, and look up at us, hoping we shall feed them. When we do take out a bucket of food they will try and scramble into it, and jump up to snatch pieces of food off the spoon. It is strange to think that once-wild people, who would soon be quite wild again if we let their wings grow, should grow much tamer than the farm-bred ducks which never knew a wild life. I will tell you about one. Late on a hot summer's afternoon, all the young ducks that had been hatched out that spring walked up to the house hoping to be fed. One poor little undersized fellow could hardly stagger along. We thought at first he must be dying of some illness. Then I had the idea that perhaps he was starving, because he was so small and weak that his stronger brothers and sisters pinched all the food before he could get any. We ran indoors and found him a crust of bread, and kept the others away as we fed him. He just sat back on his stump of a tail and gorged himself. In about ten minutes he was strong enough to totter back to the water. In about an hour, lo and behold! he was sitting outside the door waiting for more. From then on we fed him by himself until he became as much of a nuisance as a pet lamb. I really believe he would have paddled upstairs to our bedrooms if we had let him, so tame and fearless did he become. But we were rewarded by seeing him grow later into a splendid drake in all the glory of a mallard's plumage.

There are very many different kinds of wild duck and even their names are interesting—mallard, tufted ducks, teal, wigeon, pochard, golden-eye, pintails, garganeys, shovellers, scaups, goosanders, and last but not least, the eider duck, from whose soft breast comes eiderdown. (The quilt that you have on your bed is only called an eiderdown because of the down from the duck with which it is stuffed). With only small differences all ducks are much alike in their habits and in the places where they build their nests. You will seldom find a duck's nest far from water, but only one or two kinds of ducks will put it in wet places. The rest like to know that their homes are in nice dry surroundings. The nest is usually on the ground, though occasionally the mallard sticks it in the fork of a tree, and is made of dried leaves and things, lined with masses of soft downy feathers. All ducks lay a lot of eggs, anything from five to fifteen, according to the kind of duck, and these can be all called white. Certainly they are not spotted nor are they really coloured. They vary from the true duck-egg blue—a colour which I cannot begin to describe but which you will soon come to recognise—through greyish, dirty white, almost to a grubby, coffee colour. I fancy this depends a good deal on the materials of which the nest is made. The eggs just get dirty and stained. All ducks also eat much the same kind of food—that is, most of them eat almost anything which they come across—a sea-slug, a worm, a fresh-water snail, small beetles and insects they snap up in the grass, corn they pick up on the stubbles, tender shoots of rushes or water-weeds—or my lettuces! They use their flatbeaks like shovels. They fill their mouths with mud and slush and then strain it off, and swallow whatever small worm or grub may be left behind. Though I have included ducks among the birds of marshland and lake, that's because they favour such places for nesting and bringing up their families. The nearer you get to the sea the more ducks you will find feeding on the mud-flats and salt-marshes. Here the ducks of the rivers are joined by those which live near the sea—the scaups, the goosanders, and the smews. Many of those which gather there are visitors who have only arrived for the winter.

The three kinds of duck which you are likely to come across without struggling into out-of-the-way corners of the country are the mallard, the teal, and the tufted duck. We have already had a lot to say about the first. There is still much left to say, but I have only space to tell you one or two things. First, mallards in their wild state like to sleep and snooze quietly in the reeds or rushes during the day, and only come out at dusk to "flight" that is, to fly off in pairs to their nightly feeding places. Here in the darkness they eat and talk and chuckle and fly about till dawn begins to break. Then back they come to rest and digest their meal in the sunshine. Next, the drakes, as you will see, are really splendid people. Yet in summer they go for a time into what is known as their "eclipse" plumage, and become almost as brown as the ducks. Indeed, for a time you can hardly tell drake from duck, except that his beak remains yellower than that of the lady. Lastly, the tiny ducklings are a joy and a wonder to watch. Of course, they have got the most absurd figures; their round heads, set on round bodies, look like a tiny lop-sided cottage loaf on legs. They are all "rollish-in-a-ballish," if you know what I mean, and cut no sort of dash when mother suspiciously, with stiff neck and tail outspread, brings them on land. But in the water they are more like

WILD DUCK AND DUCKLINGS

water-beetles than baby birds. They don't swim, but seem to half-scamper, half-paddle. They dash really fast after flies and things, rising right out of the water as they go. They seem to be able to move far quicker than their grown-ups can swim, though this may be because they are such scraps of things.

The teal is the smallest and one of the gayest coloured of our ducks—that is to say, the drake is, because all lady ducks are drab, inconspicious little people, as becomes mothers of such noisy and unruly families. You *can* see the teal in most parts of Britain, but you are far more likely to do so if you live in the northern half of England or in Scotland. He is tiny, but a champion flier. If you disturb teal as they are feeding (they feed far more by day than other ducks), they will shoot off the water straight into the air as if released by a spring, and dash off at a terrific rate. When they have flown out of harm's way, as they think, they will shoot as quickly on to the water again, alighting with head and wings well forward. You may remember that we called a number of teal "a spring of teal"—perhaps the word comes from the way they spring off the water into the air. Teal have the most charming way of talking to one another. All ducks hold muttered conversations and chuckle to one another—often with their mouths full!—but the teal is the best talker of them all. You can hear him from quite a distance before you have even spotted him. The drake has also a musical whistling note, which sounds sweetly over the still waters of a lake or river.

The little tufted duck is staringly black and white, with a large yellow eye and a black tuft of hair, which gives him a puzzled and surprised look. I think he is really my favourite among the ducks. There was a time not long ago when he was only a visitor to Britain, but now more and more of them stay with us all the year round. You can see him, in winter at any rate, on

COMMON TEAL

almost any large stretch of water, but just as well on the ponds in the parks of our big cities. Indeed, I don't know where you will be better able to see ducks of many kinds than in London—in Hyde Park, on the Serpentine, and especially in St. James's Park, where numbers of wild ducks come to join those which are kept as tame ones.

The tufted duck is a diver, and just about the champion diver too. Unlike the mallard, he spends almost all his time on the water. For an hour or more he will just float idly, seeming to be half-asleep in the sunshine. Then he will decide he is hungry, and it is high time to hunt for some food. So, presto! he disappears. You may be able to follow him by the chain of bubbles which he leaves; but even if you can, you will be surprised where he bobs up again. Not only does he dive easily, but he goes down very deep, to the bottoms of

WHOOPER SWANS

really deep lakes and ponds which no other bird can reach. His call is a funny sharp sort of "Chrrrrr!", and he nests very late in the year—in May, or even June. In winter when lakes are freezing, you will often find a small area of open water around the tufted ducks. That is because, unless the frost is very hard indeed, the warmth given out by the little bodies of the ducks sitting on the water stops the water round them from becoming cold enough to freeze.

The last person we must mention is certainly not the least. In fact he is the biggest of all the birds of lake and pond—the swan. He will be seen just as much in town as in country—he makes no attempt to hide himself and little attempt to hide his nest—and there are few public parks in our cities which are without swans. So I don't think many of you will need to be told what he looks like. He is as large and proud as he is beautiful, and can also be very savage and dangerous when angered. Although he seems to move along with the breeze or the current, he is really paddling himself along by slow, strong beats of his webbed feet. When he is excited he gets into top-gear, and fairly charges through the water. You may know the swan quite well by sight without learning some of the more interesting things about him. To begin with, there are about three different kinds of swan which visit Britain, and the proper name of the one which you know is the mute swan. Mute is another word for silent, so it's not quite correct, because the swan does make some noises. You will probably know the sort of hiss it makes through its nostrils, and if you go near the nest when the male swan is there—and I hope you never will do so, because it really is dangerous, as the swan is very, very strong, and can easily break a boy's leg with one blow from its beak or wings, or knock a girl into the water!—he will let out a sort of grunting snort. One thing you cannot help noticing is the funny black knob on his forehead at the end of his beak. His beak is a lovely orange colour but ends in this black knob. If you ever see a swan without that black knob, and with a yellow instead of an orange beak, you will know you have seen one of the two other kinds of swan—the whooper swan or Bewick's swan. The difficulty about the ordinary swan is, that you can never tell whether he is tame or wild. So many of them have been tamed for so many years, yet fly about from one place to another, that it is difficult to say whether you should call them wild birds. When they build their great, piled-up nest on the edge of the water and in the reeds, they seem to feel that they are strong enough to protect it from prowling animals or from you and me without either bothering to hide it or making it difficult to reach. They are very devoted parents and pair off for life. (By the way, the proper name for the male swan is "cob," and for his wife "pen."). If the pen dies, the cob doesn't try and find another mate, but remains alone. When they are nesting, the cob mounts guard over the pen and her two eggs, and, as I said, woe betide any inquisitive person who tries to hunt her or steal the eggs! You may sometimes see swans in flight. They look rather odd, because they fly with big, slow beats of their wings and with their necks stuck straight out in front. As their strong wings beat along they make a drumming sound like a small aeroplane.

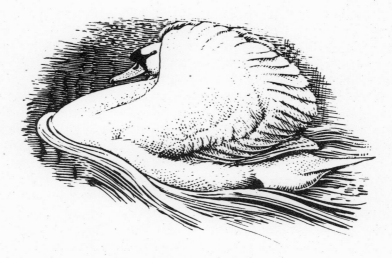

MALE SWAN BUSKING

And now the river nears the sea. As we follow it down, the reed-fringed banks broaden and become bare, until at last they are just flat and muddy, and too soft for us to walk on. Then at last, far ahead of us in the water, we can see long lines of white coming towards us, and we know these are waves, and that we are at last on the shore. The funny thing is, that birds like to go to the seaside just as much as boys and girls; but most of them go in wintertime, while we like to be there when the weather is hot and we can bathe and laze and play. Also, we usually choose the places where there is lots of warm, dry sand. The birds much prefer mud, if you please—the wetter and oozier the better. So, as you get nearer these mud-flats at the river's mouth, you will find them covered by an army of birds, which will rise into the sky with shouts and cries and whistles. You will recognise lots of old friends and acquaintances, for all sorts of inland birds visit these happy hunting-grounds. With a loud croak a heron will flap up from a pool. Plover will tumble into the air and curlew sail off, blowing bubbling noises through their trunk-like beaks. Duck may rise with a whirr of wings from the water, and even little pipits and wagtails flip up, to land again a few yards away. I couldn't begin to tell you all the different birds that you might see together. Many of them are visitors, and, anyway, until you know a lot about birds and their ways, and can spend whole days in getting close enough to them to watch them, most of the birds of the seashore will remain distant acquaintances. You may only see them for a second or two close-to, and not probably until you are grown up will you be able to go off in search of their nests on the lonely stretches of coast or high up in the cliffs.

But there are a few birds which you will be able to see on mud-flat or shingle, or even on the beach, where you spend your holidays. Of course, if you are thinking only about your bathing or of making sand castles, you won't notice anything; but if you keep an eye on the sea, you will sooner or later catch sight of what looks like a swarm of darkish-brown flies flying fast and low over the waves. All of a sudden, and all together, they flash white, and you can then see that they are a flock of brown birds which have suddenly turned and shown you their white tummies. They are dunlin, and are to be found almost all round our coasts, though you may not see them so often in the south as in the north. They are small wading birds, and you can watch them running quickly along the beach at low tide, always down at the water's edge, so as to pick up any tasty morsel as soon as the sea leaves it behind. As they run, they twitter to themselves about what they are finding. The interesting thing about the dunlin is the way they are drilled. As I have said, when they fly they all turn together as if some sergeant-major had shouted "About Turn!" to them. They will suddenly all settle on the water at once, and then you will see them just as suddenly rise into the air again and turn all together. It is most odd, and, as they fly, their little wings make a kind of rustling noise. It is no good looking for their nests on the shore, because the dunlin retires

MALLARD DRAKE AND DUCK

BLACK-HEADED GULLS

inland to the moors and high places to make its nest, which is a grass-lined scoop on the ground.

Another bird which may at first seem to resemble the dunlin is the turnstone. Was ever a bird better named! All its life seems to be spent in the shallow water at low tide or on the mud-flats, poking about with its short, strong beak, and turning up the small stones and pebbles in search of the tiny crabs and shrimps which may be hiding under them. The habit is so strong that the bird will turn over any little object that it sees, just because it can't help doing it. If you see numbers of sturdy, brownish birds running about the shore, sometimes up to the knees of their orange legs in the water, you may be fairly sure they are turnstones. Of course, you will not notice the colour of their legs until you get close to them, but this should not be difficult, because they are not shy birds, being usually too busy with their hunting to bother about you. When you are nearer them you will easily recognise them by their sharply marked black and white heads. As soon as they decide you are coming too close to them they will rise into the air, and then what a difference there is! Like the dunlin, all their underparts show up, and what looked quite a dull, brown bird, will suddenly shine as a black and white one. The turnstone is a peculiarity among our birds. Although at all times of the year he is quite a common sight on all our coasts, and especially the more rocky ones, it has never been known to make its nest here. That does not, of course, mean that no turnstone has ever done so, but just that no turnstone's nest has ever been found. And in these days when so many skilled bird-watchers are at work all

HERRING-GULL

the time, it is very unlikely that a nest would not have been found if ever one had been made in our country.

Far more colourful than either of these is the oyster-catcher—a most handsome fellow, with his black and white livery, his sturdy beak of bright orange, and his gay rose-pink legs. As he flies over the sea from rock to rock he always reminds me of a Red Admiral butterfly, which has much the same red, white, and black colour scheme. You should see oyster-catchers on most of our shores, although they are far less common on the East Coast than on the West, where in general the shores are rockier. They are company loving birds, going about in small parties and sometimes in large crowds. If the turnstone is well named, the oyster-catcher is not. He may, of course, catch oysters—if you can call finding a shell-fish, which just lies on the sea-bed without moving, "catching" it! But if he does find oysters he doesn't bother with them, because he knows perfectly well that he cannot open their tough, tightly shut shells. If you've ever tried to open an oyster you'll know that it's a job for strong fingers, a strong knife, and some skill—far more strength, at any rate, than could be exerted by a bird no bigger than a moorhen. The oyster-catcher certainly does open all sorts of other fish whose shells are not so tough—mussels, for example. Also, it easily manages to knock off the rocks the limpets, which you will find it most difficult to move at all. If it finds a shell which it can't open with its beak, it has been known—though I have never seen it—to take the shell up into the sky and then drop it on to the rocks till it smashes. The oyster-catcher, another name for which is the "sea-pie" (which doesn't mean a

pie to eat, but a black and white or pied bird like the magpie), usually makes its nest near the shore. You should look for it on the ground in a field, among the rough grasses, or even among the sand and pebbles of the foreshore. Nor is the hen oyster-catcher very choosey about the materials she uses to line her nest. She may use grasses and dried seaweed or some thrift; or she may be content with a lining of broken shells—not a very comfortable sort of thing to sit on! She lays three eggs, which are much the same colour as those of other ground-nesting birds of the shoreland—fawny-buff, with browny-black markings.

Along with these dunlin, turnstones, and oyster-catchers, you will almost always find the pretty little ringed plover, first cousin to the green plover. With his black and white collar and the black marks over his eyes and forehead, which make him look as if he was wearing goggles, he is easy to pick out on the yellow sand or greyish mud. On a shingly, stony beach he blends with his surroundings, but not so well as his eggs. They are yellowish, mottled with splodges of brown, and are so difficult to tell from the pebbles among which they are laid that you could easily tread on them by mistake. The funny thing is, that the birds go and give the show away by decorating their nest with odd bits and pieces of stone, broken shells, weeds, and sticks. If you watch the ringed plover, you will see that it runs quickly along the sands for a few yards, then stops suddenly with a jerk, which brings its head and beak down—biff—to pick up the worm or insect which has caught its sharp eye.

Then, of course, there are the seagulls—ever so many different kinds of them. The curious thing about seagulls is that in a small island like Britain we needn't really go to the seaside to see them. In days of stormy weather the gulls find the waves too rough for them to get their food easily on the water and they get blown inland. You will see them in the fields, especially the ploughland, where they will be hunting in the freshly turned earth for worms and grubs. In London and other big cities near the sea, gulls are as familiar friends as the pigeons. They are everlastingly hungry people, and eat almost anything—from a dead fish on the beach to any crust or piece of bacon-rind you may give them. They are far too hungry to be afraid of you and me, and will come swooping down out of the sky to catch the crusts you throw up for them. Watch how skillfully they catch every piece as they flap down and up again. But what a shrieking, screaming, ill-mannered family they are! The truth is, that the seagull is far nicer at a distance than he is when seen at close quarters. As they wheel in the sunshine, white and gleaming between blue sky and bluer water, they are things of great beauty. Seen on a winter's morning, wailing and mewing in the mist over Thames River, they remind us of the seaside, bringing a breath of salt air into our town lives. As they swirl screaming around the big steamers in our ports and harbours, they tell us of the long voyages over wide oceans which every British boy and girl dreams of making one day. Because we have all got the sea in our veins, we

TUFTED DRAKE AND DUCK

COMMON TERNS

cannot help loving the gulls and being grateful to them, but we could wish they had better manners as well as tempers. Almost all gulls are dirty feeders. They are the scavengers of the sea, picking up all the filth and rubbish that float on the waters; also, they will steal the eggs of other birds, and sometimes the young birds. They eat small crabs or other shell-fish, and break these open by carrying them into the air and then dropping them on to the stony shore. Lastly, they will eat farmland wheat as well as worms, and any old bit of food you can spare from your table. They snatch at their food, tear it in pieces, and bolt it in the most greedy way. Then, with their tummies swollen and eyes half-closed, they balance themselves on one leg and digest it.. If you look at that old gull sitting on the post which sticks out of the mud, you will see he has a big, cruel beak, and a fearless and cunning look. Yes, the ordinary gull is a greedy bully, I'm afraid.

The commonest of the many kinds of seagull round our coasts are the black-headed gull and the herring-gull. You cannot mistake the black-headed gull because of the sort of browny-black mark or hood over its face and head. It is very fond of coming inland, not only to feed but to nest. They make these nests of sticks and grass and rushes on the ground, and lay two to three eggs. Like those of other gulls, the eggs vary in colour. They may be a bluey green or an olive green, or buff or brown, always with splodges of black and brown on them. The herring-gull is white and pale grey, and a most beautiful flier. You must watch the way it glides and sails away up in the sky—turning, soaring, and diving without a flicker of its wings. It comes as readily as its black-headed cousin into towns and cities, ever mewing and hungry, ever on the watch with its round yellow eye for anything that a gull could call a meal. It nests in colonies, placing its nest on the grassy slopes of cliffs or on the ground. Of course, there are so many gulls that you may easily see others, including the graceful tern or "sea-swallow," which, common though he is all round our coasts, is only a summer visitor.

If you visit a rocky shore or live near one you will have lots of other birds to watch—those which nest in the tall cliffs or in cracks in the rocks. Some will be old acquaintances. There will be rock pipits, and hawks patrolling high in the sky. There will be jackdaws, and all sorts of gulls screaming and fighting to put their nests on the shallow cliff ledges. On the rocks against which the waves shatter themselves in snowstorms of foam, you will see the still, dark figure of the cormorant, most skilful of bird fishermen.

Indeed, seaside and shore are the great gathering-place for birds. Here come all kinds, great and small, to feed or to nest. Here come also all the birds—tiny, as the chiff-chaff, or huge, as the geese—which are visitors to Britain. So, remember that the sands and the cliffs and the beaches are something more than memories of a summer holiday. They are the places where better than anywhere you can see birds.

CORMORANT

Chapter VI

VISITORS

LASTLY, there are our visitors—the birds which fly over the seas to spend part of the year in Great Britain. Some, you will remember, come down in winter from the northern countries which lie deep in snow. Others come up from the south to escape the fierce heat of the African summer. Some are only passage migrants. You may sometimes have made long journeys by train. If you travel from Edinburgh to Brighton, for example, you'll almost certainly have to stay a night in London. If you go to Glasgow or Swansea from Ipswich, say, you could probably find a way cross-country, but it would be easier and more comfortable to go by London. Your labels would be marked "Passenger to Brighton (or Glasgow, or Swansea) via London." It is the same with birds. Some go from Africa and Europe via England to Norway and Sweden. Some from these northern countries via Scotland or the Scottish Isles down into Europe. They only stay with us long enough to rest and recover their strength for the second stage of the journey. They emigrate from one place to another by way of Britain, and so we call them passage migrants. What will surprise you is that counting these sort of week-end visitors and all the rare arrivals, there are far more birds which visit Britain than there are which live with us all the year round. Out of over 400 birds which have been seen in the British Isles at some time or another, only 133 are residents. Even without the passage migrants and rarities, there are almost half as many regular visitors as there are British residents. Most of the visitors are uncommon, of course, and it is unlikely that more than a few of them will become close acquaintances.

We have wandered so far away from our homes and gardens in search of the birds of field and woods and water that I think we had better go back to them, and begin with the visitors who will become our familiar friends—people who seek our company and make their homes near ours.

The cuckoo selects himself as the first of our visitors to be considered. For

DUNLIN
RING PLOVER

one thing, his cry of "Cuckoo!" is the trumpet-call which tells us that spring has come, and that the birds of the Southland have begun their invasion of our country. Most of these come silently in the dawn or at dusk, to fall breathless on our shore. They are here in force before we know it, and it is the cuckoo which shouts "We are coming! We are here!" for them all. All of you know that call of his, so musical as it floats to you on the breeze, but so loud and impudent when blared at you from close-by. The cuckoo breaks the rule about being seen and not heard. You'll find he is usually heard but not seen, though when you know what kind of a person to look out for, you'll soon spot him. He is a largish bird, grey barred with thin black stripes, a small head for his body, and a lovely long tail, which he spreads fanwise. If you see him flying he's not unlike a hawk, and, indeed, is sometimes shot at by people who don't know birds and who mistake him for a sparrow-hawk. There's a rhyme about him which goes:

> "The cuckoo is a pretty bird,
>   He sings as he flies,
>   He brings us good tidings
>   And tells us no lies."

He brings us the good tidings of spring, but I cannot say whether he tells us any lies. Certainly he does utter his "Cuckoo" call as he flies from one tree to another. By the way, it is only the cock which cries "Cuckoo." The hen is a far quieter person, who occasionally lets out a puzzling, bell-like, yet bubbling call, quite unlike that made by any other bird. There's a deal of truth in the old rhyme I set down at the beginning of this book—"In April come he will," and sometime in "August, go he must," though a few may linger on with us till September. What do cuckoos do between April and August? I'm afraid they don't behave very kindly. The cuckoo is the only one of our birds which is not only too lazy even to bother about home-building or bringing up its young, but, worse than that, pushes the whole job on to some much smaller bird. The cuckoo is the prize mystery among British birds. The hen cuckoo never makes a nest of her own. Instead she spends her time house-hunting, finding out where little birds, like hedge-sparrows, meadow-pipits, or wagtails are building their comfortable nests (remember these birds are about half the size of the cuckoo, and their nests small accordingly). Then, when she feels she is ready to lay an egg, she pops down on one of the nests she has picked out. First, she goes to the nest and carefully takes out in her beak one of the eggs the little bird has laid, and drops it on the ground. Then either she squats somehow on the nest—how she manages this is part of the mystery—and lays her own egg in it; or else she lays her own egg somewhere, carries it in her beak, and places it in the nest she has robbed. Men who are very learned about birds have spent months and years patiently watching the cuckoo in order to

CUCKOO CALLING

find out, first, how she chooses the nests in which she will put her eggs; and, secondly, exactly how she manages to get her own egg into them. Anyway, the fact is that somehow or other she does it—and then goes off to find another nest, and another, until she has laid probably six or more eggs, all in the other birds' nests. Another thing. The hedge-sparrow lays a bright blue egg, the pipit a speckled one, the wagtail a speckled one too. It is said that the cuckoo lays an egg like that laid by the bird whose nest it has chosen. Well, I can't say. But I don't think it is true. All the cuckoo's eggs I have found have been whitish, but so thickly covered by brownish spots that you could call them brown. They show up in a hedge-sparrow's nest like a bar of soap in a coal-hole, but are much the same as the other eggs in a pipit's or wagtail's nest. One thing is odd. Although the cuckoo is a bird as big as a thrush, its egg is no bigger than a sparrow's. So, whatever its colour, the little hedge-sparrow or pipit just sits on it until she has hatched it out with her other two or three eggs. What she doesn't know is that out of this egg will come a hungry cuckoo, which grows twice as fast and twice as big as her own babies. This little beast at once eats all the food the mother brings, and, almost as soon, seems to know that the food won't be enough or the nest big enough for all. So it just heaves the other babies out of the nest to die on the ground. And all the while the tiny mother-sparrow or pipit goes on feeding him, until he has become so huge that he quite overflows the nest—something like a full-grown hen sitting on an eggcup—before he flies away to join the other cuckoos as they are getting ready to leave Britain for their winter homes in Africa. The wonderful thing is that every spring and summer thousands of small birds are ready to spend all their time and energies on bringing up these ugly, greedy,

and murderous young cuckoos, which have been cunningly planted in their homes while they were not looking.

Yet the cuckoo isn't all bad. He eats all manner of insects which attack our plants and vegetables and which other birds will not touch. And what would spring be like without his ringing cry? African though the cuckoo may be, his call is as much part of the British countryside as the hawthorn blossom, the daffodils, the pink tassels on the larches and the gold on the gorse.

By the time that the cry of the cuckoo is heard in the land, most of the swallows will have arrived. Of course, if your eyes are open, you would in the previous autumn have seen those busy family gatherings of young swallows and their cousins, the martins, sitting lined in long rows on the telegraph wires, while mothers and fathers lectured them about the long journey to Africa, which they must shortly take. They make so many preparations for their departure in September that you can hardly miss them, but they come back again in March, April, or May without any fuss at all. There are three members of the swallow family—the swallow, the house-martin, and the sand-martin. All have graceful, streamlined bodies, long, sharp wings curved like a scythe, and forked tails. Except that they can't hover like the kestrel, they are proably the fastest and most expert fliers of all our birds. And well they need be, for all their food has to be caught as they fly. They have huge mouths, slits right across their faces, and these are held wide open like sacks as they dart, swoop, and turn hither and thither in the air. Their lightning-quick eyes spy all the tiny insects which hover and hum in the summer warmth. Down they go, and into their sack-mouths goes fly after fly after fly. When they have a good big bundle, so big often that odd ends of fly stick out on either side of their faces, the birds fly back to their nests and feed them into the gaping mouths of their babies. You may hear people say that when the swallows fly low it's a sign of rain. So it is, but the swallows only fly low to catch the insects which when rain is coming do not rise so far from the ground. You watch the swallows on a dry, hot day, and see how high they are hunting. Then notice how, when storm clouds are banking up or there's a smell of wet in the air, they sweep low over lake or field, often no more than an inch or so above them. Once upon a time these swallow-people probably nested in caves or niches in the rocks. Some of them still do where they can find big, roomy caverns, but, generally speaking, each now builds in a different sort of place. Swallows and house-martins are birds of our houses and homes. The swallow likes to put its nest on a rafter or some such place in barn or stable. One pair nest regularly in the old stable where my pigs live. Its rather a nuisance, because, while they are nesting, the only way they can get in is through the door, so that I have to keep it open for them. The result, of course, is that the poor pigs sometimes have to lie in a draught with the door open. It's not much of a nest they make, only a few straws and feathers, which the birds stick together with a sort of gluey spit from their mouths. (Did you ever hear

SAND-MARTINS

of the soup which the Chinese make from birds' nests? Of course these aren't ordinary nests of grass or moss or sticks or feathers, but the curious gluey nests of a kind of East Indian swallow which the birds make by sticking their spit, bit by bit, on to the walls of the caves. The Chinese collect these nests of dry glue, and melt them down and strain them for soup—and jolly good it tastes too!) The house-martin is the nest-builder of the family. He makes a beautiful nest of mud, and sticks this on to your house—if you are lucky— just below the eaves. We are lucky, because every year we have six or seven pairs of martins nesting just above our bedroom windows. We can both watch and hear them all the time from the day they begin their home-building until they all, fathers and mothers and young ones, fly away to their African homes in September. What we see first is the martins flying about round the house and in the fields. Next we notice them taking a lot of interest in the house. The little birds will fly up to the eaves, hang on there somehow by their claws, and hold excited conversations. Mr. House-martin is asking Mrs. House-martin what she thinks of this place for a nest. What she answers we can only guess, for in a day or two we can watch the two of them swooping down on to the mud round the pond or in the road, stuffing in mouthfuls of it, and then flying back to spit these muddy mouthfuls on to our house. More than half the mud they bring falls on to our window-sills, but after hundreds upon hundreds of visits the foundations of the nest begin to appear, and then one day we see that a nice round ball of mud has been stuck on to the wall, with a little opening at the top. Out of this opening pops Mrs. Martin's head, all white to the ears; up flies Mr. Martin, hangs on to the nest, and chit-chatters to her as she sits there. From then onwards till they fly away there's a continual whispering and chattering. Even if we wake in the night and ask, "What's the time?" we seem to wake them too, for that delicious, eager whispering and chattering begins at once. It's such a friendly and companionable sound, and we do miss it when the birds at last decide it's time for them to pack up and fly away. Before that, one or two young birds have managed to find their way into our bedrooms, and have to be caught and put out of the windows again. As we hold them in our hands we can see how lovely they are, with their tiny beaks, black eyes, and their white shirt-fronts. The martin isn't really as beautiful as the swallow. He is not so colourful. He has no chestnut tummy, nor such a finely forked tail, but I must confess he's one of my most favourite birds, as I expect he will be yours one day. For while he is with us he becomes more one of our family than our guest. He is all sweetness and gentleness, doing no harm to any one, and I am sorry for the way the sparrows are always trying to pinch the cosy nest he has built with so much skill and trouble.

The sand-martin is the odd man out of the family. You won't find him in your gardens or around your houses. That's because he is a tunneller rather than a builder. He makes his home in holes which he digs into the sides of any sand or gravel pit or even quite low sandy banks. You will notice that many of these pits or banks are honeycombed with holes. If you visit them in spring or summer you will see martins flying in and out of them. The birds make these holes by pecking with their beaks and scratching the sand away with their feather-covered feet. Sometimes they are content to dig in for only a few inches; at others, they will make a tunnel of three or four feet so that your arm can hardly stretch to the end of it. Just imagine all the work that means for tiny beaks and feet! The nest is a poor affair, just a packing of straw and feathers, and I'm afraid that, being built where so little air can reach it, it is usually full of fleas!

If you want to know the swallows from the martins as they fly, here are three sure signs. The swallow itself is bluey-black, with a chestnut tummy and a forked tail. The house-martin is black and white, with a white splodge where his tail joins his back. The sand-martin is much more browny, and has a bar of dark brown across his white chest. The martins also always nest in colonies, while the swallows pair off and find places on their own. Both the martins lay white eggs, but the swallow's eggs are covered with fine reddish spots. When the first chill breath of autumn stirs the drying leaves on the trees the swallows get ready to depart. They start lining up for two or three days before they go, as if they were soldiers falling in for some parade. Then one day they are off, without anyone seeing them go. But my brother once saw them arrive at the other end. He was in West Africa, and one evening his black servant rushed in to his tent and told him to come out. The black boy took him to a marsh of huge, tall reeds, and there, whistling down out of the sky and falling with a crash into the reed-bed, came millions of swallows. They went on coming for hours, and as they fell, worn out after their long journey, the tall reeds bent and broke under their weight. The thousands

SWIFTS

of small parties which had left different parts of Britain and Europe must have joined up somewhere into a mighty army of birds, millions strong.

As the swallows fly in wild sweeps you will often see high above them a bird which you'll probably think is another and larger swallow which screams as it flies. This is the swift, the most streamlined flier of all British birds. It has the same type of build as the swallows, but its scythe-shaped wings are longer and stronger, its body shorter, and its tail no more than a short rudder. Yet the swift is no relation to the swallows. He catches his food in the same way, sweeping insects into his wide mouth—it stretches even wider than a swallow's—as he flies. And as he flies he screams. At dusk he soars to dizzy heights, far away out of our sight in the gathering twilight, so far away that his harsh screams reach our ears but faintly. He's not a companionable bird, and will remain no more than a distant acquaintance, although you'll find he usually makes his home in the roof of your house or outbuildings. His nest also is made of feathers and straws glued together with spit like swallows, and in it the hen swift lays two long, thin white eggs. In olden days people used to think that the swift had no feet, and the artists who hundreds of years ago used to paint the coats of arms of princes and knights knew the bird as the martlet, and always drew it without feet or legs. Of course the swift has feet, nice little feet, feathered to the toes, but they are poor things so far as walking goes. Indeed, the legs are so short that if ever a swift lands on flat ground it has a difficult job to rise again. It can't get its wings clear of the ground to bear itself into the air, so it usually takes care to alight somewhere where it can use its splendid wings for an easy take-off. The bird which is related to the swift is that mysterious night-flier the nightjar, which we should properly not bother about in this book, because he usually flies at night, and is only found in certain parts of England. But perhaps as you are sitting and eating your suppers on a summer evening, you will hear a sort of "Churr-churr-churr" coming from some distant woodside, and you will know that the nightjar has risen from the bracken and is on the hunt for the moths, beetles, and other insects which fly in the gloaming. He's a grey, long-tailed bird, and he moves silently and ghost-like as any owl. Really he flies rather like one of those big, grey moths he loves to catch. During the day he crouches in the bracken or near stones, and his feathers camouflage him so well that he seems to melt into his surroundings. You could almost tread on him without spotting him. He is not a pretty bird. Indeed, he's got such a blunt head, short beak, and bag mouth, that when he is at rest he looks rather like a toad. One of his many nicknames is "Flying-Toad." Yet when he is flying he doesn't look toad-like at all, and, if you ever spot one in flight, I think you'll say that "Moth-Owl" is a good name for him. His commonest nickname is "Goatsucker," because long, long ago people imagined that he used to go at night and suck milk from the nanny-goats. The hen is a lazy body. She makes no nest, and just lays her two longish eggs on the ground. And very beautiful they are, polished and shiny like marble, in which shades of white, grey, brown, and purple mingle with one another.

Now we come to a large family of small birds—the warblers. I always think that they look exactly what they are—soberly dressed, modest, well behaved, busy little people. But don't think because they are so quiet and modest that they are shy. Far from it. They seem to be quite unconcerned with you or me; far too busy in their everlasting search for flies and insects— up one branch, a quick inspection of a leaf, a peck at something, and then off again. There's no hurry or bustle, but they are never still. I can see one of them—a garden-warbler—as I write this. He's examining the rambler roses outside my window. The warblers are fascinating birds, but I imagine you may find it difficult to make close acquaintances of them until you are older. Most of them are so alike and so difficult to spot anyway, that your eyes have to be well trained before you can hope to tell one from the other or know any of them well. There are a lot of them—the common and the lesser whitethroat, the reed-warbler and the sedge-warbler, the grasshopper-warbler, the willow-

NIGHTJAR

GRASSHOPPER-WARBLER

WHINCHAT

warbler (or willow-wren), the wood-warbler and the chiff-chaff, the Dartford warbler, the garden-warbler and the black-cap warbler. Most of them are plain greeny-grey birds, with only tiny points of difference between them, though one or two are quite distinct. The warblers arrive in hundreds of thousands between the middle of March and the middle of May, and most of them spread right through England, Wales, and Scotland. You won't see them arrive, but it's certain that you'll know almost at once when they have come. One spring day you'll find your attention caught again and again by small green and grey birds with delicate beaks, rather sleek heads and kindly eyes, slipping in and out of the fresh green leaves on tree or bush. However small and quiet they are, you can't overlook them, because they are so busy and so plentiful. The truth is that, although we don't realise it at the time, our woods and gardens don't fill up properly till the visitors arrive, and the warblers are important, for it is they who fill up the bushes and low undergrowth. If you have a keen ear for music you can have an interesting time picking the song of one warbler out from another. You'll hear them even oftener than you see them, and will be able, if you are clever, to tell them better by their songs than by their appearance. For as the name tells you, the warblers are all useful singers, with small tinkling voices. Only two—the blackcaps and the garden-warbler—are in the real top class.

Let's take a quick look at them.

The common whitethroat, and his small cousin, the lesser whitethroat, are true birds of fields, woodside, and hedgerows. The whitethroat is common everywhere, but the smaller bird is not found much in the north or in Scotland. Because the whitethroat can thread its way so easily through thick and tangled shrubs or undergrowth he is sometimes called the "Nettlecreeper." Both birds make their nests in much the same sort of places— in the bramble and gorse-covered banks at the edge of a wood, or in struggling overgrown hedges. You'll seldom find the whitethroat's nest more than a foot or so from the ground. It's a fairly compact one, of small roots and twigs, and is lined with horse-hair. The eggs, which may be four or five, are a curious greeny spotted colour, unlike those of any other bird I know. The lesser whitethroat nests a little higher up, but his nest is a much more flimsy affair, of thin twigs, grass, and horse-hair, often so thinly woven that you can see through it. But it's usually beautifully concealed, and very often hung just under a branch of bramble, so that the leaves act as a natural roof against rain or sun, and also hide the nest from inquisitive eyes. One Whitsunday I found twenty-one nests of the two kinds of whitethroat in about two miles of a gorse and bramble-fringed ride in Clumber Park, Nottinghamshire.

As you'd imagine from their names, the reed and sedge-warblers are birds of marsh and mere. The reed-warbler, which you will only see in the southern parts of England, ranks

BLACK REDSTART

STONECHAT

with the goldfinch, long-tailed tit-mouse, and goldcrest as a first-class nest-builder. It's not that his home is so soft and downy, but so cleverly woven and anchored. It is built of long pieces of flag, sedge, and reed, woven and twisted round the stems of three tall reeds, and lined with the soft feathers of the reed flowers or with wool. It's deep and cup-shaped, and when the hen sits in it you can only see her beak and a bit of tail over the lip of it. As the reeds sway in the wind, the whole house sways too, but it's so firmly tied up to its supports that it is perfectly safe. The funny thing is, that as the reeds grow, so the nest rises higher and higher! It must be rather like making your bedroom in a slow-moving lift! Though the sedge-warbler likes much the same swampy ground as the reed-warbler, it makes just an ordinary nest, which it builds on dry land, in a grass tussock, in brambles, or in a very low bush. You'll find the sedge-warbler almost anywhere, and he's another of those chatterboxes which are more likely to be heard than seen. When your ears are trained to bird music, you'll find that you'll often hear the sedge-warbler's song without seeing him or being able to get near his swampy hide-out, just as you will have difficulty in reaching the reed-warbler's nest.

The same thing is true of the grasshopper-warbler—isn't it a lovely name? He doesn't get it because he either looks or behaves like the acrobatic grass-hopper, but because he is supposed to have a song—if you can call such an odd little noise a song!—like the sort of clockwork noise made by grasshoppers on a hot summer's day. I don't know the song well enough to describe it to you, but I don't think it's really like the grasshopper sound at all, but far more like the noise you make when you wind up the reel on a fishing-rod. You see what *you* think it is like when you hear it. The point is that, though this warbler is not at all common, he appears far less common than he is because he is so seldom seen. Yet your quick ears may be able to hear him singing or reeling away. More even than hedge-sparrows he shuns the open, and prefers to skulk about in the undergrowth, wind himself up inside and then unwind himself—at least, that's what it sounds like.

All the warblers we have mentioned so far have ordinary cup-shaped nests. The willow-warbler, the wood-warbler, and the chiff-chaff all make domed nests—if you can call such a soft bundle of grass, leaves, and feathers anything more than a ball. The first one I ever saw was when I was very young. In our Yorkshire garden a lot of branches had been cut down. We piled these into a stockade—I think we had just been reading *Midshipman Ready*—behind which we made a sort of dug-out. One day, when we were preparing to man the stockade against Indians or pirates, we suddenly saw what we thought was a loose ball of grass and feathers stuck in the branches. We nearly pulled it out before we realised it was a nest. Then we watched and saw it belonged to a willow-warbler. The next summer we found a nest on the ground in the short grass in a meadow. The whole trouble about these ground-building warblers is that it is so easy to tread on their lovely homes; and, of course, hundreds

SWALLOWS

HOUSE-MARTINS

upon hundreds of them must be destroyed by cats and rats and stoats, and even by mice, to whom a meal of warbler's eggs would be a real tit-bit. So, if ever you see the little greeny birds—you will be less likely to see the wood-warbler —busy coming and going from a certain spot, walk warily, otherwise you may tread on their nest, which from above only looks like a little heap of leaves, if you can spot it at all. The eggs of all these three warblers are much the same—whitish, flecked with reddish spots.

The Dartford warbler is a rarity which you must not expect to see. If you do come across one you will be very lucky. I never have done, and I only put him in here because he's a bit of a freak. He's the only one of the large family of warblers which is a regular resident. He stays with us all the year

RING-OUZEL

round, though there are not many, and what there are, are only to be found in a few of the southern parts of England.

I always bracket the blackcap and garden-warblers together, because I've found their nests in the same places and once in the same bush. The garden-warbler is really no more fond of gardens than the blackcaps—or, for the matter of that, the willow-warbler or the chiff-chaff—but I've nearly always found them in the shrubberies of big gardens or in the same sort of garden trees growing in plantations or woods. They are both very fond of box-trees, but will put their nests in almost any evergreen, in rose-bushes sometimes, or in brambles. The nests are both made of twisted grasses, a few roots, and lined with hair. The eggs of both birds are rather lovely. They are richly marbled eggs, and you'll always be able to tell one from the other if you remember that the darker egg belongs, rightly it seems, to the blackcap, which is the darker bird. Indeed, the blackcap is the only one of the warblers you'll be able to recognise as soon as you see him. The name suits him perfectly. But I'm not so sure you'll see him as often as the garden-warbler, which is almost

SPOTTED FLYCATCHER

certain to become a close acquaintance. You'll hear both birds more than you will see them, and splendid singers both of them are. Many bird-lovers think that the blackcap is only beaten by the nightingale, and, indeed, it is sometimes called the "Northern Nightingale," because it is found almost all over Britian, while the nightingale never struggles farther north than Yorkshire, if it gets as far.

The nightingale is, of course, the champion of all birds which sing or warble. Here I must let you into a secret. I had always thought that the nightingale was a warbler, and it was only the other day I learnt with surprise that he is no relation at all, but a distant cousin of our old impudent friend the robin, and through him a member of that very large family, the thrushes. Perhaps if I had had many opportunities of watching the nightingale I should have seen that he resembled a robin in the way he stood, with legs planted sturdily apart, his tail raised, and his head cocked sideways. But the trouble is, that the nightingale is one of the most retiring of all birds. He seldom ventures far away from the deep undergrowth of wood or thicket. Here he makes his nest, finds his food, and in summer pours forth that gurgling, varied song which has become so famous all over the world. I'd like to know what you think about it when you hear it, and whether you consider its all that much better than the lovely vesper hymn of the blackbird, for example. I have an idea that the real reason the nightingale's song is so famous is because he sings it at night. He has the stage to himself. The summer dusk has fallen, and the loud day-time songs, chirps, squawks, and cries of a million birds are stilled. An owl may hoot, perhaps, or the quack of a duck echo from a distant pond, but except for such-like occasional noises, there is silence over the country-

side. This silence is shattered by the loud, liquid singing of the nightingale. Certainly he has a long song, and puts every ounce of his energy into it, but remembering that he has no competition, and that music often sounds better in the darkness, I believe he would find his championship in danger if only we could train the common blackbird or one of the warblers to perform at the same hour of night. Anyway, you hear him—you'll be more likely to do so if you live in the southern part of England—and see what you think. The nightingale does sing also by day but then his voice is only one among so many that it does not stand out as a solo performance. There used to be a belief that the nightingale never slept, and there is a lovely old legend about its watchfulness. Once upon a time, so runs the tale, the nightingale and the blindworm had only one eye apiece. When the nightingale was invited to the wren's wedding, he was ashamed to show himself with one eye, so he waited till he caught the blindworm asleep and stole its eye. The blindworm said: "When I catch you asleep I will get my eye back!" "Will you?" answered the bird, "I will take care never to go to sleep again." So, because the nightingale goes always in fear of being caught asleep, he keeps singing both by day and by night. If you wish to find the nightingale's nest, you must seek it in the thick undergrowth in the wood near where you hear him sing. It will be placed low down in brambles or a thick bush, and the eggs you'll find are olive-brown, rather like much smaller pheasants' eggs.

There are a lot of interesting and handsome relations of the thrushes and robins among the spring visitors. Among the birds of the open spaces are the ring-ouzel and the chats. You may remember I warned you that the ring-ouzel was nothing like the water-ouzel or dipper. He is just a blackbird with a white collar, which lives on the moors or rocky hillsides instead of in gardens. You will never see a blackbird on very high ground nor a ring ouzel on the low land. But on the moors of Yorkshire, Derbyshire, on Dartmoor, and the mountainsides of Wales or Scotland, you'll be sure to see them. And where you see them, there, deep in the heather near one of the tiny mountain streams, you'll find their nests—just like a blackbirds, even to the mud lining. Even the eggs are the same, except that both the blue-green and the reddish spots are deeper in tone.

In much the same sort of places as you see the ring-ouzel you should also see the perky little stonechat. Where the moors are crossed, as in Yorkshire, with grey stone walls, or where rocks jut out from the heather, you will see the stonechat hopping along the walls or from rock to rock. He will go farther down into the valleys, where between the heather and the meadows there is, maybe, a fringe of gorse and bracken. It is in the gorse chiefly that the hen makes her nest, very low down in the bush. The nest is not unlike a robin's, and the eggs are somewhat similar, except that they are blue-green, splodged with reddish-brown instead of white with reddish-brown. On the top of a gorse-bush, swaying in the wind, will sit the little stonechat, and if you go

REED-WARBLER
SEDGE-WARBLER
WHITETHROAT

RED-BACKED SHRIKE

near he will shout "Tzchack! tzchack!" at you—a sharp noise, that has been well described as like that made by striking two pebbles together. It is this sharp cry which gives him his name of chat. The stonechat is not only a visitor; many are all-the-year-round residents in Britain, though they come down from the hilltops to escape the full blast of winter.

Just as the blackbird is the lowland ring-ouzel, so you might say the whinchat is the lowland stonechat. When you say whinchat, you think at once of the furze and brambles of downland or common, just as stonechat puts you in mind of the rocky uplands where the birds live. So, too, I think the plumage of the two birds seems to point to the stonechat being the sturdier, hardier person, and the whinchat the summer visitor from warmer climes. Whether you will see the whinchat or the stonechat will depend a lot on where you live. Just as the stonechat likes to perch up on walls, rocks, and gorse bushes, the whinchat will perch on a shrub, or a tree or a telegraph wire. I've usually found the nest in much the same sort of places as the stonechat—chiefly at the bottom of a gorse bush. Even the nests are alike, and the only difference in the eggs is that the spots on the whinchat's eggs are smaller and paler, perhaps, than those of the stonechat's.

Another relative from Africa which inhabits much the same country as the chats is the wheatear. He is probably easier to spot at a distance because of his greyish jacket, the black streak over his eye, and, above all, by the white patch on his rump and the white top to his tail. You'll see him all over Britain on open spaces, whether high moors or lowland commons. Near my home is a wide, sandy breck—we call it—which is covered with wheatears in spring and summer. If we drive across it in a car we don't disturb the birds so much as when we walk, and we can see them flitting about from tussock to tussock, bobbing and bowing to each other, but never keeping still for a moment. The wheatear likes to live in colonies, and the favourite place for its nest is an old rabbit-hole. It is made a foot or so down the hole, not a very neat affair, built of grass, roots, feathers, and rabbit-fur. The five to six pale-blue eggs are much like those of a starling. It is good to know that wheatears are another species of bird whose numbers are increasing. In olden days they were eaten, "potted wheatears" particularly being a great delicacy, and the greedy people of those times thought nothing of eating two or three dozen of the birds at one meal. They "sucked them down and sighed for more." In order to catch the birds more easily, they even made artificial rabbit-holes on the Downs and set a trap in each.

What the chats and the wheatears are to open spaces, another relative, the redstart, is to the woodlands. I can best describe the redstart as a robin with a red tail, though that is not quite enough. If you see him you will notice that the feathers on his tail are a bright scarlet. He seems to know that his tail is something to be proud of, for he is for ever flicking it about, up and down, or from side to side. He's not a common bird, though you are quite likely to see him in any part of Britain, particularly in parklands or those open type of woods of old trees. It is in cracks or holes in these ancient gnarled trunks that you'll be most likely to find his nest, though you may sometimes come across it in an old wall or quarry. The nest is very much like a robin's, but the eggs are blue. You might at first mistake them for a hedge-sparrows, but you'll see the difference if you compare the two.

I must tell you about the black redstart. Not many years ago this was one

STONE-CURLEW

of the rarest of the visitors to our country. It was rarer even for one to be seen here, and it was practically never known to have nested in England. But now many pairs are nesting regularly, and some of them, of all places, in the bombed ruins of the City of London. There, among all the broken bricks and rubbish, the blackstarts, as they are sometimes called, have begun a permanent settlement in Britain. Expert bird-lovers can't quite explain why this should be. Some people say that the blackstart likes nothing better than rubbish and nettles to live among, and that the reason he never came here before the war was that our country was too trim and tidy for him. Then the blitz on London and other cities provided just the sort of wilderness that he liked. Other people say it's nothing to do with the bombing, but that the bird was for a long time gradually becoming more and more attracted to the British Isles, and that he suddenly decided to come over here and settle. Whichever is right, the fact is there. To-day the black redstart is a regular Cockney, nesting within sound of Bow-bells, when but a few years ago there wasn't a reliable record that any had ever nested in Great Britain.

All these chats, wheatears, and redstarts are eater of insects and flies. Some of them are quite good at catching flies in the air, considering that neither their bodies nor their wings are designed for such work. For really expert flycatching we must go to the flycatchers proper. There are two of them which visit us—the spotted flycatcher and the pied flycatcher—but the pied one is so uncommon that I don't think we need bother about him here. The difference between the flycatcher and the other insect-eating birds is that he catches all his food as he flies. In this, of course, he is like the swallows, the swifts, and the nightjar. They rush swiftly through the air in great headlong sweeps, carried, now down, now up, on their strong, curved wings. They are swift, smooth fliers. Not so the little flycatcher. Watch him. There may be one sitting on a garden fence, on the tennis net, or a railing. There he sits for a minute or so, watching, his crest fluffed up as if he were puzzled. All of a sudden he hops into the air, does a quick jerky little flight, twisting this way and that, then back to his perch again—with his mouth full of flies. He's a close-quarter hunter, not a long-range one like the swallows. Each time he makes one of his short, zig-zagging flights he manages to catch several flies. That's why he twists and jerks, so as to catch those he spies on either side of him. Flycatchers are most attractive people. My garden is full of them, and it seems a lucky one for them, too, for they manage to bring up nearly all their young ones. The one that has nested in the dead ivy near my pig-house has brought off her family for three years running. The flycatcher normally makes its nest on a wall in ivy, in creepers or trellis-work, though it may sometimes put it in a cleft in a tree, or just in the fork where a branch juts out from the tree trunk. As the flycatchers are almost the latest of the spring arrivals it is not surprising that they are about the last of the visitors to get their nesting over, and you may often find nests with eggs in them in July

WOOD-WARBLER
BLACKCAP
WILLOW-WARBLER

BRAMBLING

and with young ones quite late into August. The eggs are white, with heavy reddish spots, not unlike a robin's, though, of course, the two birds are not related at all.

Lastly, there is that other late arrival, the red-backed shrike—often known as the butcher-bird. When you see him, your first thought will be how handsome he is. Then you'll probably notice the cruel hook of his beak and his sullen look, and you'll recognise him as a killer. He is a killer, with a very wide choice of victims. He behaves rather like one of those brigands who live in wild places and pounce upon any peaceful travellers who may pass by. What the shrike does is to take up a good position on a bush, a hedge, or a post, and then settle himself to watch. Quite still he sits, except for his head, which swivels from side to side as he looks all round him. Almost any insect, bird, or animal which is not too big for him to tackle, is fair game to the shrike. He will dart from his perch after a passing fly, beetle, or bee, or swoop down on mice or small birds. Or he may change his manner of attack and go ranging down a hedge like a small-sized sparrow-hawk, ready to pounce upon any small thing which runs, or creeps, or flies. He will seize baby-birds from their nest, and eat a nice meal of lizard just as happily as a young pheasant. But he doesn't kill his victims so swiftly and cleanly as the hawks. He usually carries them back to his post or perch and then carves them up with his beak. Bigger creatures like field-mice or small birds may have to be hung up somewhere convenient before they are carved, and it is this unpleasant habit which gives him his name of butcher-bird. He will carry mice, birds, beetles, or bumble-bees back to some thorn tree or bush, and stick them each on a thorn. Then he can cut them up as he feels inclined. Some people say he makes a larder of the creatures he has killed round his nest, so that his wife will have a meal within reach whenever she needs to feed her young ones. Certainly all the shrike's nests I have found have been in thorn bushes—usually the big, overgrown, single trees that grow on commons and open places; but I've never found what I could call a proper larder. All I've seen were the remains of two or three beetles —just their horny shells—and perhaps a bumble-bee. Still, as you can understand, the shrike is not a pleasant bird, except in appearance.

GREY LAG GEESE

There are, of course, many other interesting visitors which come to Britain to make their summer homes, but these are either rare birds like the wryneck (a snake-like person, who is often called the cuckoo's mate) or the stone-curlew, otherwise known as the thicknee (because of his ugly shaped legs) or Norfolk plover. Or they are birds which keep far away from the places where you are likely to go regularly. Anyway, it wouldn't be correct to put either the rare visitors or the out-of-the-way visitors in your list of friends and acquaintances. You must look forward to adding them gradually.

It's rather the same with the winter visitors, though there are not so many regular winter arrivals as there are spring ones. Only twenty-six kinds of birds come to us each winter from the northlands, and most of them are birds of the mud-flats and lonely shores, places which you are hardly likely to visit between the mists of autumn and the mad blustery days of March—by which time most of them will be winging their eager way northward again to make

their nests. You must understand that the winter birds come to friendly Britain in order to find food which they could not obtain in their own countries, where the earth is iron-hard with frost or buried deep in snow for weeks and months on end. Unlike the spring visitors, they do not choose each their own little patch of garden, field, wood, or river, and then set up house close-by, and stay put all spring and summer while they build their nests, hatch off their eggs, and bring up their young ones. No! They come to find the food, berries, roots, grain, or grubs which they can't find in their homelands, and they roam about in search of these from one district to another. They just follow their noses, if you understand what I mean. Wherever they think there's the likelihood of a good meal, there they go. So they don't give you anything like the same chance to see them at close quarters—unless they are half-dead with hunger and too weak to bother what happens to them—much less to learn their true characters. It's a pity, because there are not a few interesting and attractive people among them. There's a very handsome member of the finch family—the brambling or bramblefinch. When I was young I had a lovely cock brambling in my aviary. The pity was that he came to a sticky end, because I had not learnt then enough about birds. I caught a great tit one day and put him in with the brambling, and in next to no time the beastly tit had bashed in the brambling's head! But while I had it, I was able to watch from close enough to see its rich black and chestnut colours, with a sort of spotted effect on its back. All you are likely to see are flocks of bramblings foraging in the winter fields among equal numbers of chaffinches, and at a distance you'll not easily pick one bird out from the other. They are very like chaffinches in their shape and in their habits.

In the same fields you'll see large flocks of speckled breasted birds—thrushes, you will say, and you'll be right. But they will be more than one kind of thrush. Some will be your old friends—song-thrushes; others will be visiting relations—fieldfares and redwings. If you saw either a fieldfare or a redwing in a cage, or held one in your hands, you'd soon learn to know it from the ordinary British song or mistle-thrushes, but I'm almost sure that for a start you'll not be able to tell one from another at a distance. Yet our fields, and even our parks and gardens, are full of these northern visitors every winter.

And if you could get up before daylight on a winter's morning and sally forth across the steel-grey waters of a salt-marsh or river-mouth, you'd hear the air loud with the cries and calls of visiting ducks and geese. You are more likely to see strange visitors of the duck family than you are to see the wild geese. For the true setting for wild geese is far from the loneliest human dwelling—out on the marshes or mud-flats. There is something mysterious about geese—these great wary birds, which come down in the darkness on our shores out of the frozen northland. Listen to what a great lover of the geese has to say: "Their flight is swift and their formations fill the sky, but I believe their greatest appeal is to the ear. When the north-east wind blows at dawn,

REDSTART

WHEATEAR

and the flood-tides creep in across the mud, it is the sudden call of the geese, half-heard above the roar of wind and waves, that brings the greatest thrill of all. When the full moon rises over the marsh at dusk, and the creeks are brimful; when eyes are strained to see which way the bubbles float, so that one may know if full-sea is past or yet to come, it is the call of geese which makes one's heart leap." Perhaps you may live on one of those lonely stretches of shoreland which are the favourite haunt of the geese. Perhaps, on some winter's afternoon, you have heard the wild calls and the beat of wings, and, looking up into the darkling sky, have seen the geese flying in a long, irregular line or "skein," or in a V-formation, as they made their way to their resting-places on mud-flat or sandbank. Perhaps early next morning you have seen them flighting back to feed on some stubbles or potato fields miles inland. If so, you will be one of the lucky ones, and one of the few, for it is not given to many to see geese except the wild-fowlers, who lie out all night with their guns waiting to shoot any that come within range.

The largest of our wild geese is the grey lag, and, except that he is altogether swifter and more streamlined, he is very like the ordinary goose you see waddling about the farmyard. Indeed, the grey lag is probably the ancestor of the farmyard goose. The grey lag, with his cousins, the pinkfoot, the white-fronted, and the bean goose, are known as "grey geese." The grey geese have similar feeding habits and are fond of inland pastures, stubbles, and ploughland. Two other visitors are the brent and the bernacle goose, sometimes known as "black geese." The brent is the smallest of our geese and is very dark in colour, his head and neck being coal-black, except for a little white patch on the side of the neck. The bernacle is a slightly larger bird, and is perhaps the most elegant of the wild geese. The black geese do not move so far inland to feed as the greys, but hunt the coast, the flats, and

BERNACLE GEESE

CANADA GEESE

the saltings for their food. By the middle of April all the geese have left us for their nesting grounds in the far north, and you will have no chance of seeing them again till late September or October. "But," some of you may say "I have seen wild geese flying in V-formation in mid-summer." You will be quite right, but the birds you have seen will be Canada geese. The Canada goose, as its name suggests, is a North American goose, which many years ago was brought into England by people who wished to keep it on their lakes and ponds because of its beauty. As the years passed, the Canada geese bred and nested and grew in numbers, until gradually they became real British wild birds. To-day it is possible to see flocks of them on many of the inland waters of Great Britain at any time of the year because the Canada goose has learnt to nest here and stay with us all the year round. Sometimes they can be a nuisance. Near my home are some water-meadows, on which pasture a large herd of Friesian dairy cows—those black and white ones, you know. In autumn the farmer scatters cartloads of mangolds over the meadows for the cows to eat. Every now and then two or three hundred Canada geese arrive, and I have seen them following the cart at a discreet distance and eating the mangolds before the cows have had a chance to get at them! That's because the artful birds know that the owner of the land is a great bird-lover, who will not have them shot, or even shot at. Still, it's a bit rough on the farmer, isn't it?

The geese, I am afraid, are birds which you will not be able to get to know well until you can set off, all properly clad, to seek them out in their own haunts and study them at close quarters.

In fact, it all comes to this. There are dozens and dozens of different kinds of birds, regular residents as well as visitors, which do not give boys and girls much chance to get to know them. Yet right at our doors, or not so far away from them, we've got quite a rich enough variety of birds to occupy us for a long time, until we can grow up and go in search of the others who are more shy or more uncommon. If you begin right, by learning all there is to know about your friends at your back door, or the acquaintances you can fairly easily make in fields, woodlands, marsh, and shore, you'll find it much more interesting when you are old enough to go out on your own, determined to add fresh acquaintances to your visiting-list.

YOUNG CUCKOO

Chapter VII

BIRDNESTING

HOW, you may well ask, can I start to learn about birds? I'll try and tell you. To begin with, it will mean training yourself to look about you all the time you are out of doors. Whenever you walk along a road or in the park you should be watching, and saying to yourself: "That was a mistle-thrush on that holly-tree," or "I think that was a yellow-hammer which flew into the hedge a few yards away." Or you can ask whoever is walking with you: "Did you see the linnet on that gorse bush we passed?" or "the cock pheasant strutting about in that stubble field?" You can even play a sort of game when you are out on a walk with brothers or sisters or friends. First, you can have a competition to see how many birds each one of you notice, and then how many of them you can recognise by their names and families, and see who wins. But the important thing is somehow or other to get the habit of observing birds so that at last it becomes second-nature for your eyes to miss nothing. When I was a very little boy my mother used to take me out for walks, and all the time she'd be showing me things—not birds only, but butterflies and moths, and beetles and toadstools and flowers. At first I saw nothing unless she stopped to point it out, but gradually, I too, found I was looking for things—birds and beasts, and flowers and fungi, all the time. And not only when I was walking, because it's just as easy to spot birds from a car or even from the windows of a railway carriage. The first thing, therefore, is to see that your eyes are wide open and watchful.

The next thing is to make up your mind to go out in search of birds. Now some of you may not perhaps mind living in big cities and taking your walks along hard, grey pavements. Perhaps some of you, like Christopher Robin, may think: "It's ever so jolly to call out ' Bears,' watch me walking in all the squares!" Perhaps, indeed, some of you are quite resigned to those sedate promenades in a party of "Grandpapa, mamma, and me, the poodle and the pug." Well, of course, you'll never find out about birds in these ways. What

117

you must do is to persuade your fathers and mothers, governesses, teachers, or friends, to take you across the fields, down lanes, through woods, or over commons, where you know you'll be sure to meet some of the friends and acquaintances we've talked about. And especially in spring and summer when they are nesting, and you can try your skill at finding their nests.

Bird-nesting has got a bad name. That's not because it is wrong, but because of the wrong way in which so many boys and girls—and grown-ups, too, I'm afraid—used to go about it. Bird-nesting should mean finding the nests and eggs of the birds, not smashing the nests and stealing the eggs. If you ever go bird-nesting you should always remember what I told you at the beginning of this book—that you are just about the only real friends the birds have, and that you must therefore be most careful how you venture near their homes, so that you do not harm them or cause the mother-birds to desert them.

THRUSH'S NEST

Another thing. Bird-nesting often means torn clothes, scratched legs, and muddy, wet feet. So you may possibly have a hard job to coax your elders into letting you do it as often as you get the chance. But it's worth trying, because, however tired, scratched, dirty or wet you may get, you'll find by going bird-nesting that your walks and rambles will be so much the more interesting in themselves, and also that you'll come to know birds so much more easily and quickly.

There are many ways of setting about bird-nesting. The bird experts are most scientific. They know that a certain kind of bird whose nest they wish to find has been seen, or may be seen, in a certain district. So away they go to the place, and hunt around either till they see or hear the bird they are after. You see, they know its colour, its habits, and its song as well as the reflection of their own faces in a mirror. It may be they have spotted a hen-bird. If so, they sit back and watch her through their field-glasses as she goes to and fro building her nest or carrying food for her babies until they know exactly

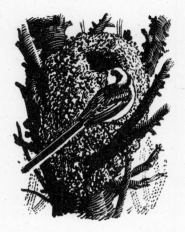

LONG-TAILED TIT AND NEST

where her nest is, and can walk straight to it. Or they may hear the cock bird singing. Then they track him down, and watch him in the same way till he hops down to talk to his wife on her nest. It's much less trouble, of course, to find nests that way, but you can only do it after you have learnt such a lot about birds. Also, I fancy, you'll find more fun if you begin by just going and hoping to find some nests, any nests, even one nest, no matter to what kind of bird it belongs.

I think you'll start by just prowling round your own garden or a neighbouring park or field, as soon as spring has started to drape the dry boughs with enough tender leaves to give the birds shelter and cover for their nests. You'll find your eyes will first spot the big, coarse nests of blackbird and thrush, stuck in the fork of a thorn or laurel bush, or in the ivy on house or wall. Later you may come across the oddly placed home of a robin in an old boot or can. But you'll probably find this by accident; and then, by the time the trees and shrubs are really covered with leaves, the cosier, more beautiful, and better-

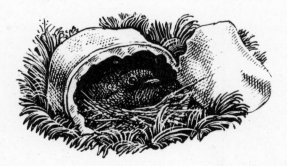

ROBIN'S NEST IN A CAN

hidden nests of hedge-sparrow, chaffinch, and yellow-hammer. Each year we make close inspections of our garden, bush by bush, and ivy-covered wall by ivy-covered wall. Then, when we think we have found all the nests in it, we stumble the next week across one we had quite passed over. And when winter comes and the leaves fall again we always find several nests which we never discovered at all during summer. There is one pied wagtail which I'm sure, just comes on to the grass in front of our windows to wag his tail and laugh at us. We know that each year he nests somewhere quite close, but so far we've never found his nest. Of course, we've never really watched his movements, but we have hunted in all the likely places.

The next thing I think you will do is to go for hikes and rambles especially to hunt for nests. You put on old clothes and you go out into the fields or over the moors or commons, poking or peering into all the hedges, bushes, brambles, or even nettle patches, you come across. You don't get along very fast—that is, you don't cover many miles, but you do have fun, and aren't you tired when you come home! And haven't you a lot to talk about! Perhaps you wish to walk a long way and yet to find nests as you go. Then the best way is to walk along with a stick and give the hedges or bushes a light bang with it. If a bird is sitting on its nest, this bang will usually make it fly out, so that you then know where to look without bothering about all the bushes in which their are no nests.

Bird-nesting gives you all the exercise and fun of finding the birds at home and seeing how they live and what their eggs are like. It also gives you lots of wonderful experiences to remember. There'll be the thrill of finding your first cuckoo's egg, for example. It was on a Whitsunday morning before breakfast that I found my first one. I and another boy had got up early and push-biked to a private lake not many miles away. There we clambered through brambles and shrubs to find a mallard's nest, all dry leaves and downy feathers, under a laurel bush. As we peered through the branches of the bush at this nest, there, right under our noses, was a neat little hedgesparrow's nest, with three bright blue and one brown egg! How we jumped for joy! We didn't stay to look for any more nests, but fairly rushed home with that cuckoo's egg. We felt we had saved the hedge-sparrow a lot of worry and trouble by taking it. The funny part of the business was that that same evening we actually found a second cuckoo's egg in another hedge-sparrow's nest, this time in a hedge. That was a big thrill too, but not quite the same as the first one.

There are days, many days, when you won't find a nest, not even in the most likely of places, or when you may go down the hedge at one side of a field and draw a blank, and still find lots of nests in the opposite side. There are other days when you'll find all sorts of nests you never dreamt of finding, and some of which you may not be able to recognise till you've gone home and looked them up in a book. Only the other day I found a nest low-down in a

FIELDFARE

REDWING

COOT AND NEST

bramble covered field-hedge. It was a grass-and-wool nest, and it had six little bluey eggs with tiny red spots. It ought to have been a linnet's, but the eggs looked both too small and too blue. I took an egg out, and sent it to a friend in London who knew lots about birds. He told me it *was* a linnet's, but that the eggs were probably the first ones laid by a very small bird, and for some reason, too, they were much bluer than the usual linnet's eggs.

But the day which stands out in my memory is a pouring wet summer afternoon in Norfolk. I was grown up, but my two sisters and my youngest brother were still at school. We all sallied forth in macs and old clothes to find what we could find. Over the brecks we went, and into big woods, where pines and firs were mixed with oaks and ash and thorn and many other green trees. We just couldn't stop discovering nests. First there were greenfinches, chaffinches, and linnets, and one without eggs we rather suspected might be a redpoll's. Then there was a plover's, and, oh, joy! a stone-curlew's with its two eggs of quite different colour. On the edge of the wood in the bracken we found a wood-lark's nest with eggs. Then we got well into the wood—we were all well soaked through by this time too!—and found two or three gold-crests' nests hanging under the branches of pine and fir trees. We found pheasants' eggs, and, of course, blackbirds' and thrushes' everywhere. At last we came to a thick part of the wood, and up a short pine tree we spied a biggish

YOUNG THRUSHES

nest. We thought it might be a mistle-thrush's or a jay's, but anyway, my younger sister said she'd go up and see. As she began to climb, my other sister had been poking round the bottom of the tree. We heard her say she'd found a rabbit-hole—and then things happened in a hurry! The sister up the tree shrieked: "Oh, there's a great big owl"—and got no further, because the bird flew out suddenly in her face and she fell down the tree! At the same second the sister on the ground screamed: "Oh, there's an owl in the hole looking at me!" And she got no further, because she fell over backwards as that bird flew out too! When they had picked themselves up and we had all stopped laughing we pieced together what had happened. It was this. The rabbit-hole was the home of Mrs. Tawny-Owl who had been sitting peacefully on one

SPOTTED FLYCATCHER ON NEST

egg when we all arrived. Up at the top of the tree Mr. Tawny-Owl had been roosting, on guard over his wife. My sisters had blundered straight into both birds, which in their fright had just flown out in their faces, frightening the girls in their turn. That was a wonderful afternoon, although we did all reach home for tea in a very muddy and bedraggled condition.

You must be careful when you go after the birds of river and marsh. Often you will see the nest of a reed-warbler, a moorhen, a grebe, or a coot, which looks so close you feel sure you could reach it. Be careful! Those nests are often farther out than you think, and what looks like dry land may be no more than a floating tangle of reed-roots or weeds, with quite deep water underneath. You try and walk out to the nest. The first few careful steps may be all right, but then, all of a sudden, splodge! and down you go. Listen to what happened to me when I was quite grown up and ought to have known better. Remember that the water-birds all nest early in the spring, sometimes when the weather is still cold. One bright March day I went out with a small boy and a dog— one of those dachshunds, or "sausage dogs." We were not really bird-nesting, but as we passed a small pond we spotted a coot's nest full of eggs. It seemed to be so close that I rashly said I'd go out to it. Out I went, followed by the "sausage dog." The first few paces were safely taken—the water came over my boots, but that was all. Another step, and in I went up to my middle in icy water! In went the dachshund, too, yelling with fright at his cold bath! All I could do was to crawl back to the bank, chilled and dripping, carrying a squirming, shivering sausage of a dog with me. We were five miles from home, and I had to take off my pants and socks and pedal home on my push-bike as hard as I could to keep myself warm. That was a lesson to me. Let it be a warning to you.

Finally, let's end as we began. Remember always that birds are people, most of whom trust you to be kind to them. Look for their nests whenever you can, but never forget these are their homes, made by loving care and much hard work. So, if to get near them you have to break down boughs or branches or rushes or reeds, don't do it. Those broken branches or reeds mean as much to the bird as if you had broken down the doors, gates, or windows of the home of one of your friends. Never spoil the sheltered or well-hidden place in which the bird has placed its nest. Never poke clumsy fingers into a nest. The bird may easily take alarm and desert it. Above all, never take out eggs without the greatest care. Remember, small fingers are not always the most gentle. A bird's egg is a most fragile thing, and will break easily unless your fingers are trained to handle it. After all, to a tiny bird, you are a huge giant, and your hands, small though they may be, are great clumsy hams. So, to begin with I should, if I were you, take advice and help from grown-ups. You'll find lots of them know a whole heap of things about the birds you wish to see, and will help you to get to know them.

All that I can tell you is, that the more carefully you go in search of your bird friends and acquaintances, the better you will get to know them, and the happier they will be. And the happier your bird friends are, the happier you will be to have them round you.

THE END

BIRDHUNTING CAT

INDEX

125

LAPWING'S NEST

HEDGE-SPARROW'S NEST